Praise for *Love Is Liberation*

"During the global crises of our time, we all need an ethical place to stand. The deep wish of the Venerable Thích Nhất Hạnh was for the human race to arrive at a global ethic: an ethic that anyone of any spiritual path could feel at home with. The Five Mindfulness Trainings are the Buddhist contribution to this ethic. The more people who have access to the Five Mindfulness Trainings, the closer we are to the collective awakening that the world needs. This book helps bring this Buddhist contribution to a global ethic to a wide audience and makes it clear that mindfulness must always be Right Mindfulness, not a means to making more money or being more successful but a means that gives us a place to stand ethically in this confusing world."

—**Bhikshuni True Virtue** (Sister Chân Đức), Plum Village France

"*Love is Liberation: Five Contemplations for Daily Ethical Living* offers a grounded and compassionate invitation into ethical reflection as a daily practice. The contemplations are clear, accessible, and quietly powerful—supporting readers to meet life with greater awareness, integrity, and heart. This is a meaningful contribution to the ongoing work of inner and collective liberation."

—**Ruth King,** author of *Mindful of Race: Transforming Racism from the Inside Out*

"How do we choose to love in a world steeped in violence and injustice? In this fresh and profound rendering of Buddhist ethical teachings, we are guided through contemplative trainings that help us respond wisely to the polycrisis of our times. At heart, these teachings are inspiring, hopeful, and empowering. They remind us of the preciousness of this living world, our innate belonging, and the transformative power of awareness and love."

—**Tara Brach,** author of *Radical Acceptance*

"In this timely update on the timeless ethical teachings of the Buddha, Brown and Gomez present wisdom grounded in both evocative raw experience—from profound new losses to old wounds, from marginalized identities to the universality of broken-heartedness—and clear-seeing at the intersections of rising oppression and accelerating change. You hold in your hands fresh perspectives on simple yet profound practices for living well together. Savor and serve them forth."

—**Rhonda V. Magee,** JD, emerita professor of law and founding director, Center for Contemplative Law and Ethics, University of San Francisco School of Law, and author of *The Inner Work of Racial Justice: Healing Ourselves and Transforming Our Communities Through Mindfulness*

"*Love is Liberation* presents the authors' contemplations as a gift that supports the Mindfulness Trainings. A generous roadmap for deeper practice, hewn from the base of the original teachings of the Buddha and Thích Nhất Hạnh, adapted for new generations of practitioners at this unsettling time for our planet."

—**Sister Peace,** Buddhist nun in the International Plum Village Tradition

"*Love Is Liberation* is a wise and timely offering that bridges personal healing and collective transformation with remarkable grace. Valerie Brown and Marisela B. Gomez invite us into a practice of mindfulness that does not turn away from injustice, grief, or division. In a time when we can so easily become disconnected from the realities of suffering and destruction, this book offers a powerful antidote to spiritual bypassing, grounding us in compassion, courage, and deep interdependence."

—**Kazu Haga,** author of *Fierce Vulnerability: Healing from Trauma, Emerging Through Collapse*

"The words 'we are purposed and we are in choice' stood out as strong medicine to help us choose life and love. Buddhist teachers Brown and Gomez demonstrate how to explore our lived experiences and find in them the earth upon which to see challenges as portals to transforming our lives.... The book is filled with good lessons on how to swim through difficult times."

—**Zenju Earthlyn Manuel,** author of *Opening to Darkness*

"*Love Is Liberation* offers the experience of narrative healing and an expansive invitation for us to live into the fullness and the integrity of life. Through deeply personal life stories and experiences, we feel into how we, as diverse and unique beings, can aspire and manifest the goodness inherent in our humanity."

—**Larry Yang,** author of *Awakening Together: The Spiritual Practice of Inclusivity and Community*

"In *Love Is Liberation,* Valerie Brown and Marisela B. Gomez offer something rare: a living, breathing ethics for our most broken and beautiful times. Their Contemplations—alongside the Five Mindfulness Trainings themselves—help us answer the deepest questions of our lives: How do I live? What is the world asking of me? How do I hold grief, anger, and joy in the same hand? It is their powerful reinterpretation of the Trainings through a lens of social justice and healing from racism that makes this possible.… With creative exercises and reflective prompts woven throughout, the authors invite us to write our own contemplations, to embody the Trainings, and to integrate them with our lived experience. A North Star for anyone seeking to walk the path of true love, peace, and liberation."

—**Kaira Jewel Lingo,** coauthor of *Healing Our Way Home: Black Buddhist Teachings on Ancestors, Joy, and Liberation*

"Dharma teachers Valerie Brown and Marisela Gomez humbly and confidently walk us through their practice of the Five Mindfulness Trainings. They offer a powerful witness in the application of these trainings as two Black women in a world fragmented in the wake of COVID and the murder of George Floyd. They illustrate their own practice with honest and human examples of how to live a life of goodness while the fire of birth and death is raging. I was touched, moved, and inspired by this offering that supports our collective liberation."

—**Drs. Larry Ward and Peggy Rowe-Ward,** coauthors of *Love's Garden: A Guide to Mindful Relationships*

"In a time of polycrisis, *Love Is Liberation* is the precise medicine we need—marrying the Five Mindfulness Trainings with unflinching social truth, it is a healing balm and a call to action."

—**Sensei Wendy Dainin Lau,** MD, author of *Inner Practice of Medicine*

"Zen Master artist Thích Nhất Hạnh, like Lady Mahamaya, gave birth to countless bodhisattvas with a multitude of liberating skills in countless realms. Liberators Brown and Gomez have chosen this realm and time to demonstrate how seemingly simple teachings become bodhisattva-like embodied wisdom. This wisdom is their teacher-theorist-artist palette for reinterpreting and applying ancient teachings in contemporary and brutalizing contexts. Brown and Gomez use an interdependent methodology to reveal the mutually-reflecting precious gems revealed when we combine the ancient and contemporary, vast planetary geographies, and various forms of oppression into the alchemizing crucible we call Dharma. Please accept this invitation to connect and reconnect with the Five Mindfulness Trainings."

—**Pamela Ayo Yetunde,** ThD, author of *Casting Indra's Net: Fostering Spiritual Kinship and Community*

"*Love Is Liberation* arrives as a precious gift in an era of compounding crises—war, climate collapse, authoritarian governance, and the daily grinding weight of racial and social injustice. Dharma teachers Valerie Brown and Marisela B. Gomez bear witness to how their teacher Thích Nhất Hạnh's mindfulness trainings live, breathe, and move through their own lives. This is a heartfelt, moving book—one to sit with, to return to, and to practice with, both alone and in community. Love is action, and we are called forward to free ourselves and our society."

—**Chan Teacher GuoGu,** author of *Essence of Chan*

"Valerie Brown and Marisela B. Gomez have written an essential guide to ethical living in these times of injustice and violence. Writing with clarity and deep compassion, their commentaries and engaging examples guide the reader toward practicing a more mindful and peaceful life."

—**Chris Mohr,** Religious Society of Friends (Quakers)

"An incredible book. Deep, clear, and rewarding, this book will surely expand readers' understanding of the essential teachings of the Buddha."

—**Heather Lyn Mann,** author of *Ocean of Insight: A Sailor's Voyage from Despair to Hope*

"Who better to guide us through the Five Mindfulness Trainings than Dharma teachers Valerie Brown—a survivor of childhood trauma and profound adult loss—and Marisela Gomez, who was left immobilized by long COVID. Together, they ground Thich Nhat Hanh's teachings in hard-won dignity, offering a living journey through each training. A luminous reminder: even in a world thick with suffering, a life of compassion and precepts is not only possible. It is the way."

—**Valerie Mason-John,** author of *First Aid Kit for the Mind*

"In this series of contemplations on the ethical foundations of the bodhisattva path, Brown and Gomez deliver a powerful wake-up roar! With deep reverence for blood ancestors and ancestral wisdom teachings, they offer an unflinching look at the polycrises of NOW. With hard-earned wisdom grounded in their own lived experience, they show us all a way to fight injustice with love, grounded in interbeing, for the inclusive liberation of all."

—**Dzung X. Vo,** MD, author of *The Mindful Teen: Powerful Skills to Help You Handle Stress One Moment at a Time*

"We all seek guidance and support in chaotic times that are too often shaped by the absence of a moral compass and manifestations of greed, anger and delusion. It is lovely to find spiritual friends and texts that can help us address the sadness and suffering in ourselves as well as the racism, militarism and materialism that has pervaded our culture to cause escalating harm. We need north stars and compasses that can guide us. Seasoned coauthors Valerie Brown and Marisela Gomez have prepared a wonderful exploration of Thich Nhat Hanh's approach to engaged spirituality in the context of a Beloved Community. You'll enjoy and benefit from their efforts. Let's keep this exploration growing!"

—**Jack Lawlor,** Dharma teacher in the International Plum Village Tradition since 1992

"Do you want to know how to live during this difficult time? These two Buddhist teachers share their stories and the basic ethical principles which guided them to clarity. This book can help you no matter your religious beliefs. Follow their paths to love and freedom."

—**Dori Middleman,** MD, psychiatrist and codirector of the Pennsylvania Gestalt Center for Psychotherapy and Training

"Valerie Brown and Marisela Gomez's book is an offering of love and courage to speak truth to what is unspoken and unspeakable. They invite us into the vulnerability of our heart-to-heart connection and homecoming for healing and collective liberation."

—**Yuk-Lin Renita Wong,** coauthor of *Sharing Breath: Embodied Learning and Decolonization*

"Everyone should read and practice with this book! *Love Is Liberation: Five Contemplations for Daily Ethical Living* is a breath of fresh air, a deeply moving, inclusive, and practical guide for daily ethical living in these challenging times, as essential as previous commentaries on the Five Mindfulness Trainings by Thich Nhat Hanh, *For a Future to Be Possible* (1993) and *The Mindfulness Survival Kit: FIve Essential Practices* (2014). In these times of individual and collective heartache, polarization, dehumanization, and polycrisis, *Love Is Liberation* encourages deep looking and deep listening. These Contemplations on the Trainings are an essential contribution in these times, inviting as they do a deepening inquiry and practice with the pivotal life questions reflected in our daily living action choices—*How should I live? What are my values? What is the world asking of me?*"

—**Lyn Fine,** Dharma teacher in the International Plum Village Tradition since 1994

"What I love most about this book is the humanness expressed by Valerie Brown and Marisela B. Gomez through their personal stories. They serve as wonderful models for trying our best to serve others and live a life of love. While precepts are not always one-size-fits-all, the authors demonstrate that love is what truly matters and that it is the glue that binds us. By grounding these principles in our shared fragility and humanity, they show us what it means to lead a well-lived life. Just as the authors write, I encourage you to approach this book with lightness in your heart and with forgiveness, compassion, and mercy for your own fragility."

—**Mark A. Putnam,** MD, medical director of Berkshire Psychiatric and Behavioral Health Associates, PLLC (Berkshire Wellness), medical director of Department of Psychiatry, Pennsylvania State St. Joseph Medical Center, and coleader of Pennsylvania Gestalt Center

"Valerie Brown and Marisela B. Gomez, two long-standing leaders and beloved teachers in the field of spiritual growth as a practice of social justice, gift the reader insightful reflections on Thích Nhất Hạnh's teachings and a compassionate analysis. In this moment of collective grief and polycrisis, their book invites ancestral hopefulness and wisdom that we can all tap into. Through their storytelling, they welcome us into their intimate and personal learnings rooted in love, heartbreak, connection, eldership, and realness about the work it takes to find our true selves. This book is encouragement for practitioners like me, a guide full of wisdom to carry as I journey in becoming a better partner to myself, my family, community, and the work in this beautiful and painful world that demands our collective healing."

—**eli tizcareño ortiz,** organizational consultant and training director with the US Federation of Worker Cooperatives

"*Love Is Liberation* is a courageous guide for these hard times, calling us to live with truth, love, and integrity. Valerie Brown and Marisela Gomez write from what they have lived, showing us that strength can remain tender, vulnerability can be power, and the world does not get the last word on who we are. With wisdom born of practice and struggle, they invite us toward wholeness, beloved community, and the freedom that only love can bring."

—**Brother Pháp Lưu,** coauthor of *Hiking Zen*

"I have been deeply grateful and moved by the authors' immeasurable minds of love from the first day they met Thầy and the Sangha till the present moment. I read each page of *Love Is Liberation* with great respect and love in my heart. The book invites people to implement the Five Mindfulness Trainings and Contemplations in daily life and, of course, waters seeds of courage, strength, love, patience, and inclusivity."

—**Sister Bội Nghiêm,** Buddhist nun and Dharma teacher in the International Plum Village Tradition

LOVE IS
Liberation

LOVE IS *Liberation*

Five Contemplations *for* Daily Ethical Living

Valerie Brown and
Marisela B. Gomez

Parallax Press
BERKELEY, CALIFORNIA

Parallax Press
PO Box 7355
Berkeley, CA 94707
parallax.org

Parallax Press is the publishing division of
Plum Village Community of Engaged Buddhism, Inc.

Text of the Five Mindfulness Trainings courtesy of
Plum Village Community of Engaged Buddhism

Cover design by Katie Eberle
Interior design by Maureen Forys,
Happenstance Type-O-Rama

Printed in Canada by Marquis

Parallax Press's authorized representative in the EU and the
EEA is SAS Plum Village at Home—Point UH, 437 Chemin du Pey, Thénac,
France | Email: europe@parallax.org

ISBN 978-1-967175-17-8
Ebook ISBN 978-1-967175-20-8

Library of Congress Cataloging-in-Publication Data
Names: Brown, Valerie (Educational consultant) author | Gomez, Marisela B., 1965- author
Title: Love is liberation : five contemplations for daily ethical living / Valerie Brown and Marisela B. Gomez.
Description: Berkeley : Parallax Press, 2026. | Includes bibliographical references. | Summary: "A courageous call forward from BIPOC and LGBTQIA+ Buddhist practitioners to transform the cycle of racial, ethnic, and social suffering through ethical choices and action from a place of belonging and love-the ultimate liberation-in this companion to Thich Nhat Hanh's Five Mindfulness Trainings"-- Provided by publisher.
Identifiers: LCCN 2026024392 (print) | LCCN 2026024393 (ebook) | ISBN 9781967175178 paperback | ISBN 9781967175208 ebook
Subjects: LCSH: Spiritual life--Buddhism | Buddhist ethics | Meditation--Buddhism
Classification: LCC BQ4302 .B76 2026 (print) | LCC BQ4302 (ebook) | DDC 294.3/444--dc23/eng/20260521
LC record available at https://lccn.loc.gov/2026024392
LC ebook record available at https://lccn.loc.gov/2026024393

1 2 3 4 5 MARQUIS 30 29 28 27 26

Contents

Introduction 1

1. Our Journeys to This Moment 13

2. Living into the Five Mindfulness Trainings . . 37

The First Mindfulness Training: Reverence for Life 38

The Second Mindfulness Training: True Happiness 42

The Third Mindfulness Training: True Love 47

The Fourth Mindfulness Training: Loving Speech and Deep Listening 52

The Fifth Mindfulness Training: Nourishment and Healing 57

The Five Mindfulness Trainings Deepen All Other Wisdom Teachings 63

The Five Mindfulness Trainings Cultivate Our Internal Guidance 70

3. Living the Contemplations on the Five Mindfulness Trainings 79

Contemplation on the First Mindfulness Training: Acknowledging Beauty as Reverence for Life 87

Contemplation on the Second Mindfulness Training: Belonging and Connecting as True Happiness 94
Contemplation on the Third Mindfulness Training: Cherishment as True Love 103
Contemplation on the Fourth Mindfulness Training: Vulnerability as Deep Listening and Loving Speech 111
Contemplation on the Fifth Mindfulness Training: Welcoming as True Nourishing and Healing 117

4. Practicing the Five Mindfulness Trainings and Contemplations Together 123
Reflection Practices 124
Creating Your Own Contemplations 129

5. Five Practitioners Offer Reflections on Living the Five Mindfulness Trainings and Contemplations 133

Appendix: Dharma Resources 149
The Four Noble Truths 149
The Noble Eightfold Path 151
The Four Establishments of Mindfulness 157
The Six Paramitas 157
The Five Spiritual Powers 160
The Four Immeasurables 164

Notes 167
Acknowledgments 171
About the Authors 175

Introduction

Marisela:

The Contemplations on the Five Mindfulness Trainings emerged from our individual and collective heartache as well as the aspiration to feel reconnected to the Trainings and their vital ethical framework for living in difficult times. As long-term practitioners, we had heard over the years that some folks from marginalized groups felt distant from the timeless language of the Five Mindfulness Trainings and the assumption that we all have the basic conditions to practice them. During 2020's dual catastrophes of the global COVID-19 pandemic and the unlawful killing of another Black body, viewed worldwide on our screens, followed by a summer of global protests to address militarized state violence, this gap seemed to widen in our hearts. Our heartache—a mix of grief, rage, mourning, loss, erasure, alienation, anger, and fear—grew from what was happening in the collective consciousness as well as our own lives. As mindfulness practitioners who know that wisdom and clarity can come from acknowledging difficulties without shame, Valerie and I took the space and time to sit together, to reflect on what was arising in our hearts, and to open up to how the current events, if openly acknowledged, might help to reconnect those of us who felt distant from the Trainings and the love and liberation they offer. For example, when anger or rage arises, if it is acknowledged, embraced, and explored without judgment, it can lead to greater clarity, understanding, energy, and eventual transformation and healing. We realized we could call on the Mindfulness Trainings' potential to turn what could be poison into healing.

With the Five Mindfulness Trainings as our foundation, we cocreated the Contemplations to invite in a broader or more inclusive understanding for ourselves and those who were not "feeling it." Writing the Contemplations, our commentary on the Five Mindfulness Trainings, we realized that we were also granting ourselves permission to deeply reflect on the words of our community's teachings and apply them to our lived experience. Through writing together, we found ourselves sharing this sense of freedom to study and practice the Trainings with others around us. We realized we could call on the Mindfulness Trainings' transformative potential to turn what could be poison into medicine.

This book is intended to share the conditions that ushered in this writing process and share our personal experience and insight realized through the practice of both the Five Mindfulness Trainings (referred to as the Trainings in this book) and the Contemplations on the Five Mindfulness Trainings (referred to as the Contemplations). The Contemplations are not intended to usurp or replace the foundational teachings of the Five or the Fourteen Mindfulness Trainings, which were profoundly and generously offered by Zen Master Thích Nhất Hạnh and the Plum Village community.

Transmitting the Dharma is one of the greatest generosities to ourselves and to others, particularly in spaces where it may not have landed previously for reasons of access. We never intended that the Contemplations would "rewrite" the Trainings; instead, they were meant as a commentary to connect the Trainings to lived experiences of systemically marginalized peoples during a time of multiple crises. Several years later, here we are, still in the midst of an extended set of multiple crises for humanity and nature—what some call *the polycrisis*.

To name all the elements contributing to the atmosphere of this time in which we have written the Contemplations would require this entire book, but listing just some of the more prominent aspects here seems relevant. We invite you to take a deep breath in and out here, to ground yourself in stability and freshness, and repeat as needed after reading each sentence describing these elements.

In February 2022, the Russian Federation launched a military invasion in Ukraine and war ensued. Three years later, the US Center for Strategic and International Studies reported approximately 320,000 Russian and Ukrainian military personnel dead.[1] One year after Russia invaded Ukraine, 1,195 people were killed and 251 Israeli hostages were taken by Hamas and other militant groups in Palestine, and the forces of Israel retaliated, a continuation of an almost century-long system of occupation and apartheid. Today, as of the publication of this book in 2026, the genocide of the Palestinian people continues. According to the United Nations Office for the Coordination of Humanitarian Affairs, in 2025, two years after operations began,"1,200 Israelis had died, and 5,431 were injured; through retaliation attacks by the Israeli armed forces against Hamas in Gaza, 61,158 Palestinians had been killed, and 151,442 were injured."[2] Also in 2025, Sudan and the Democratic Republic of the Congo have been at war, resulting in a humanitarian crisis and millions of people being displaced. In 2026, the decades-long conflict between the United States, Israel, and Iran erupted into open war, and the outcome of this violence will reverberate for many more generations.

Since his reelection in 2024, the 47th president of the United States—the most powerful country in the world—has been putting in place authoritarian governance with few or no checks and balances by the legislative and judicial branches. This has resulted in the elimination or downsizing of several federal government departments; in 2026, the subsequent job losses numbered more than 300,000.[3] Legislation that will decrease federal subsidies in housing, education, income, and health care for the most needy people in the United States has passed both legislative branches. The effect is already and will continue to be devastating for many.

The current federal administration has engaged in a wholesale dismantling of diversity, equity, and inclusion (DEI) measures, which had been put in place by private corporations and federal, state, and local institutions to encourage more diverse workplaces, address historical underrepresentation and systemic inequities in many fields (like education, law, and science), and promote the flourishing of innovative ideas. As we write, the US Supreme Court has ruled to limit the Voting Rights Act and dismantle Black congressional districts, thus ending a major Civil Rights achievement and harkening back to 1877 and the end of the Reconstruction era.

Just as devasting are sweeping efforts, again by the federal administration, to dismantle every office and every program designed to protect and defend the civil rights of Americans. The civil rights enforcement arms of federal agencies, including the Social Security Administration, Department of Education, Office of Environmental Justice, Department of Veterans Affairs, and the Department of Justice, have all had their budgets slashed or eliminated entirely. While our civil rights still exist on paper, we no longer have effective enforcement mechanisms to protect and defend these rights. In the Department of Justice (DOJ) Office of Civil Rights—often considered the crown jewel of the DOJ—some have estimated a 70 percent reduction in attorneys in that office alone.[4]

Additionally, there is a continuing attempt to minimize the historical significance and legacy of the United States' exploitation of Indigenous peoples and its enslavement of African Americans. Mixed into this refusal to recognize the United States' history of genocide and oppression is continued colonialism, anti-Blackness, extraction of Indigenous people's land and waters, and attacks on queer, transgender, and non-binary people—specifically seen in the withdrawal of health services for trans people and the denial of their humanity. Large-scale deportations of undocumented people have been ongoing, shocking in their arbitrary cruelty. Terrorizing tactics by immigration officials against communities of color—kidnappings, concentration camps, indefinite incarceration, the persecution of political activists, and even murder—are reported with increasing frequency. These severe deviations from the ideals of democratic governance upheld by the United States in the past, along with the reluctance in public spaces to acknowledge the effect of racial capitalism (the interdependence of racism and capitalism), has resulted in worldwide fear of a continued decline in the United States' participation in any form of democratic leadership broadly—and global environmental stewardship specifically.

Government policies that protect the environment have been eliminated, moving us closer to catastrophic climate changes. The current federal administration has significantly weakened or rolled back environmental regulations covering emissions, water, and wildlife, marking one of the largest deregulatory efforts in US history. Specifically, in 2026, the Environmental Protection Agency revoked the "endangerment finding," the legal basis for federal climate regulations. Add to this the various threats to human livelihoods and democracy itself presented by artificial intelligence and we understand we are living in a time of truly unprecedented peril.

This is a *polycrisis*: multiple crises that are interconnected and global. While we are not currently in a viral pandemic like COVID-19 in 2020, we are in a continued pandemic-like state of oppression and extraction by those in power across the world. In the midst of these crises, we invite our community to come back home to the Five Mindfulness Trainings and the Contemplations. Together, they acknowledge the suffering that is present and share ways to move toward ending this suffering. In a time of greater normalization of greed, aversion, and delusion, the Trainings and the Contemplations offer us a steady guide that keeps navigating us back to our values, our path of understanding and love. In a society that publicly normalizes injustice as the way forward—injustice being the foundational way power dominates those without power, forming a network of oppression that connects all the elements of the polycrisis—historically marginalized people will suffer more. The Buddha taught in the first of the Four Noble Truths that suffering exists. And, not all suffering is equal. Some of us, because of the color of our skin, our immigration status, our gender, or our sexual orientation, may suffer more. Therefore, it is even more urgent that we mindfully find ways to acknowledge this truth and take care of it. We can take care of our hearts to assure they do not harden while we build our compassion and strive toward staying inclusive of those harmed and those causing harm. Everyone has a role to play, because everyone is directly or indirectly affected; we are not separated in this network. That is, how we show up can either add to or dilute the existing chaos. We are in choice—and how lucky are we to have choice in growing our love as our path of liberation.

Over the years since we first wrote and offered the Contemplations to our community, we have received feedback and reflections on their use from individuals and *sanghas* (spiritual communities) in the US and internationally. We are happy to know that studying and practicing with the Contemplations, individually and in sanghas, has helped people better understand one another. Of great importance has been the feedback from folks in marginalized groups that their ability to connect with the Five Mindfulness Trainings was enhanced through reading and reflecting on the Contemplations. Perhaps like a road leading toward the Trainings, the Contemplations have brought people closer to them. For this we are happy and grateful.

Following the writing of the Contemplations in 2020, the ARISE (Awakening through Race, Intersectionality, and Social Equity) Sangha was the first to offer a wider public platform for their consumption. We remain grateful for this, and we would like to take the opportunity at this writing to clarify a common misunderstanding about the origin and source of the Contemplations. While publicized by ARISE, and now often identified as "the ARISE Contemplations," they were in fact not created by the ARISE Sangha. We have a strong and deeply committed relationship with the ARISE Sangha, and we are grateful that ARISE has included the Contemplations with other resources on their website. After review and engagement with leadership in the Plum Village community, *The Mindfulness Bell* magazine also published the Contemplations. We remain grateful to all of these early supporters for sharing their platforms and allowing the Contemplations to reach many people.

We hope that our shared experiences will help you practice with the Trainings, interpret them, and write your own contemplations and commentaries on them as a way of studying them and going more deeply into their meaning. Together, the Contemplations and the Five Mindfulness Trainings themselves continue to help us take good care of the pain of the past—especially the suffering that surfaced during 2020, the year when we wrote the Contemplations—and the current moment, which continues to be chaotic and oppressive for many of us. While the suffering caused by the actions of the powerful in US society is intensifying—through systems that are increasing the normalization of racism, xenophobia,

Islamophobia, homophobia, transphobia, classism, elitism, patriarchy, misogyny, climate crisis, and authoritarian governmental regimes that continue to directly and indirectly fuel hatred and division—we must actively cultivate and engage with our compassion and joy. In fact, our openness and commitment to positivity is essentially the basis for how we change the harmful, oppressive path that our society is on, nationally and globally. We hope that you can use these ethical guidelines as your North Star, guiding you through a path of practice leading to clarity, love, joy, and understanding. While this book was written by US-based folks, we understand that what we do in the US impacts the world, that we live in an interconnected and interdependent world, and as we live into our values and moral codes—our spiritual practices—we know there is no separation. Therefore, this book is for the global community, as we find our way forward through an understanding that cultivates the path of true love and peace and liberation.

A NOTE ON LANGUAGE We use several terms and phrases that have come to represent a shared understanding in the United States of groups to which we belong. This includes the phrase *people of color*, which denotes people who identify as non-white. In the United States, BIPOC is an acronym used to designate Black, Indigenous, and People of Color. We use the word Black to designate groups inclusive of people who are Black-descendant: African American, Afro-Caribbean, Afro-Latinx, etc. LGBTQIA+ is an acronym to designate several gender and sexual identities: Lesbian, Gay, Bisexual, Trans, Queer/Questioning, Intersex, and Asexual; the plus sign indicates others not named. We recognize that people use different terms and phrases to designate groups depending on the country and culture in which they live; our intention in using these terms is for clarity and is not intended to limit the application of any insights we may offer.

A NOTE ABOUT THE TITLE OF THE BOOK Thầy (teacher in Vietnamese) Thích Nhất Hạnh says that to love is to understand, and writer and activist bell hooks assures us that love in bloom is an action. This book centers our aspiration to live with love as a foundational presence in our world. The word "love" can have many meanings and is highly charged. When we speak of love, we mean to ease the suffering and to support the well-being of all sentient beings. Love, for us, is the act of caring deeply for others as we would for ourselves, excluding no one. Love motivates our actions and our work in the world, which is for the benefit of all beings.

We live in a highly individualistic society in the United States, one in which the ancient Asian roots of mindfulness have become commodified and secularized by consumer culture. In this process, the ancient roots of the Buddhist precepts are delinked from their ethical and moral underpinning of social good. Too often mindfulness is "sold" as a lifestyle or a tool for personal liberation from any and everything that ails us. This contributes to the false notion that liberation is a self-help, individualistic achievement. We use the word "liberation" to acknowledge that the nature of liberation is communal. We live in an interconnected and interdependent world. Our liberation affects your liberation—and that affects the liberation of all beings. As the civil rights leader Fannie Lou Hamer once said, "Nobody's free until everybody's free."

To have ethical guidelines or precepts that bring us back to a path of love is our path of liberation; to have a community to remind us when we forget—*this is the path of collective love, collective liberation.* Loving is liberating ourselves from our suffering, and in so doing, we release others to their journey of liberation. We are invited forward, together.

HOW TO USE THIS BOOK You are "in choice"—this book is an invitation— and we are so happy you are here. You can read this book straight through or you can turn to any one of the Five Mindfulness Trainings and accompanying Contemplations that have heart and meaning for you, and begin there. We do encourage you to engage the reflective practices located in Chapter 4. We are aware that one size doesn't fit all, and you are a unique and unrepeatable expression of you. Please consider how these Contemplations fit into your life. We hope that you feel heard, seen, and understood. Although we have done our best to be as welcoming and inclusive as possible, we may have fallen short, and we want to acknowledge that there might be language that is activating for some readers. We offer this trigger warning to be mindful that it is neither possible nor wise to write a book that will not activate or trigger anyone, anywhere.

As you read this book, please take good care of yourself: pause, breathe, go for a walk, listen to music, have a cup of tea, dance, shake, gaze at a flower or leaf, or lean into whatever supports are available to you. Consider reading this book with your spiritual community, your sangha, or a close friend.

Our hope is not only that you will personally read, study, and engage with this book, but also that you will do this in community with others. Practice stopping, pausing, calming, resting, listening, healing, transforming, understanding, and looking deeply—and not just into your own views and the views of people who agree with you. **Seek out and engage in this practice with people you don't know well and people who may disagree with you.**

Our hope and aspiration is that this book dismantles walls between differences and ultimately serves as a bridge, uniting you with people you know and people you don't know, connecting us all on the path of understanding, love, freedom, and peace.

May this book offer a way into a system of ethics for your everyday life and guide you on your path of liberation.

1

Our Journeys to This Moment

Valerie:

Grief and love are deeply interconnected, and it was my experience of both that led me to write the article "Contemplations on the Five Mindfulness Trainings: A New Paradigm for Racial Justice and the Global Pandemic." I began writing in 2019 as I supported my brother, Sam, month after month during his treatment for chronic heart failure, which eventually led to his death in February 2020. I was not only grieving his death, but I was also mourning the end of my ambiguous and complicated fifteen-year marriage. This was followed by desperate months of quarantine, isolation, and physical distance due to the COVID-19 pandemic. Each day revealed new and disturbing information about the disproportionate impact of COVID-19 on Black, Latinx, and Indigenous people, immigrants, elders, essential workers, and low-income communities. And then came the police killings of George Floyd, Breonna Taylor, and others; the worldwide and national protests calling to defund the police; and the expansion of the Black Lives Matter movement. As each event cascaded into the next, I instinctively turned to to the Plum Village mindfulness practice and teachings.

Months before, I had visited Blue Cliff Monastery, a mindfulness practice center in the Plum Village lineage in upstate New

York. Just as I was about to walk to the front of the Great Togetherness Hall to offer a Dharma talk, a nun had approached me and given me a copy of the Sutra on Transforming Violence and Fear.[5] I turned to this sutra to help me understand my own feelings and the colliding events within the United States and beyond. I read and reflected on the sutra almost daily. Then I began reading the Third Mindfulness Training on True Love because love seemed distant and inaccessible, especially in light of my divorce. Each day, line by line, I read and reflected on this Training and this sutra in the presence of my brother's death, the global pandemic, and the social upheaval happening all around me.

To support my healing and deepen my understanding as a new Dharma teacher, I attended an online training program, Buddhist Healthy Boundaries, by the Faith Trust Institute. I learned the fundamentals of healthy and appropriate boundaries and self-esteem in spiritual teacher-student relationship; the impact of appropriate versus inappropriate boundaries in promoting effective teaching; and the guidelines for developing appropriate boundaries and necessary self-care strategies. During the program, I began to reframe my beliefs around power. As a Black woman, I realized that I was overly identified with my non-dominant social group identity and saw myself as lacking power, agency, and self-esteem because of it. The course came at a time when I was feeling particularly powerless, and it helped me to acknowledge the presence of power in my life and work and to understand power dynamics in the student-teacher relationship.

Shortly after my brother died, protests for racial justice in the United States spread rapidly, with calls for a worldwide reckoning on race in the United States and other countries. I participated in a two-hour virtual healing gathering for BIPOC, led by Ruth King, a respected teacher in the Theravada tradition and author of *Mindful of Race: Transforming Racism from the Inside Out*. It was sponsored by Liberate (now called The Village), a mindfulness app designed for BIPOC. Hundreds of people gathered, expressing grief, rage, and anger. I felt confusion and anger in me as I listened to the speakers. And then Ruth King asked a life-changing question: *How do you fight injustice without hating?*

The question became a bell of mindfulness for me. I continued to read and reflect on the sutra, the Third Mindfulness Training, and this powerful question. I began to think deeply about the meaning of power, power dynamics, and how to offer my power more skillfully and in greater service to others. Interestingly, my Dharma name is *Chan Tang Luc*—True Sangha Power, or True Power of the Sangha. A Dharma name is a personalized name given by a teacher to a student upon their ordination or taking precepts, symbolizing the practitioner's unique spiritual path. After I received this name at the Fourteen Mindfulness Trainings ordination ceremony in 2003, Sister Chân Đức approached me and said, "Power is not what you think it is." That stayed with me. I have come to understand that she was referring to the Five Spiritual Powers that Thầy articulated in his book *The Art of Power*: faith, diligence, mindfulness, concentration, and insight. (See page 160 for more on the Five Spiritual Powers.)

With all this in mind, the Contemplations on the Five Mindfulness Trainings emerged. I was motivated to write them to understand and make sense of my feelings of numbness, loss, and grief, as well as my outrage over the social upheaval occurring at that time. I spoke to Marisela Gomez, a dear friend and mindfulness practitioner who is now a lay Dharma teacher, and we agreed to write an article. The last time we had written an essay together was in 2015, after a white supremacist murdered nine Black worshippers at the historic Emanuel African Methodist Episcopal Church in Charleston, South Carolina.[6] We wrote that essay to better understand our feelings, as a path of self-healing and self-love, and to offer love and support to others who were feeling rage, terror, and so much more.

Sometimes to truly heal from loss and grief, we need to come face-to-face with a difficult truth, with regret, pain, and old wounds that are asking for a second chance to be lifted up, woven back into our life, cherished, and welcomed home. At times, my life has felt like a long process of coming to terms with a series of losses that led me to seek inner healing and inner peace. In a roundabout way, I was being invited toward forgiveness, peacemaking, and compassionate action, to live and love in the direction of kindness and vulnerability. Yet a period of profound personal losses combined with the events of the time brought me to a place of tender fragility, fear, and anxiety. I leaned on my many friends and family members—and still do.

I was especially supported in this healing process by reciting the Five Mindfulness Trainings, sometimes called the Five Wonderful Precepts, as well as the Fourteen Mindfulness Trainings of the Plum Village tradition founded by Zen

Master Thích Nhất Hạnh. These Trainings, which I also refer to as precepts throughout this book, were offered by the Buddha to his monastic and lay followers as clear guidance to lead an ethical, mindful, and joyful life. Thích Nhất Hạnh has described these precepts in countless books and worldwide teachings as a way to cultivate a peaceful and harmonious life.

The Five Mindfulness Trainings help us answer pivotal life questions:

How should I live?

What energy do I want to bring when I enter a room?

How do I act under the circumstances?

What inner guidance informs my behavior?

What are my values?

What is the world asking of me?

Our individual responses to these questions are shaped by our life experience, our values, and sometimes by our energy, health and well-being, and so much more. Whether we are aware of them or not, each of us probably already lives by a set of precepts, or principles and values. Many of us are guided by common precepts such as truthfulness, honesty, and refraining from stealing and cheating. From a tender age, we are taught these ways of becoming "good citizens" in the world, in the workplace, in our family, and with ourselves.

Some people take these precepts through formal vows, such as codes of school or religious conduct. For many, though, these vows can become wooden, flat, perfunctory, and then forgotten over time. We "set and forget" them and then feel bereft from inner guidance when we most need it. So how do we bring these precepts, this internal guidance system, into our daily life and call on them when we need them the most?

Over the years, in attending retreats with Thầy and the Plum Village community, I have come to understand that the precepts are not linear. Instead, each precept connects and is interdependent with all of the precepts. For example, the first precept on reverence for life is interdependent with the fifth precept on consuming mindfully. Since they are all interwoven, practicing one precept will impact your practice of the others. Not only are the precepts interconnected, but we are also interconnected to each other and all the elements in the cosmos. Because of all this, and because our actions have an impact on others whether we are aware of it or not, when you practice the precepts, you are not doing so for yourself alone, as a separate entity—you are doing so for all beings. What you consume and how you consume will have an impact on yourself, on others, and on the earth.

According to Thầy's teachings on emptiness, your body isn't just yours; your body belongs to your parents, society, and future generations. All of these have come together to manifest your body, including the trees, the clouds, and the oceans. Your body and your practice are manifestations of the whole cosmos. To practice the precepts is to support not only yourself but also your ancestors, your parents, future generations, and society.[7] To practice the precepts is to recognize this interdependent relationship between you and the cosmos. The precepts are about cultivating conscious awareness and connectedness, especially now, in a society that has gone numb with divisiveness, too-muchness, and too-fastness.

On the other hand, some people view the precepts as an unattainable set of rules that set too high a bar and are a joy killer of personal habits and preferences accumulated over a lifetime. Some say the precepts don't take into account the real struggles people face on a daily basis and the temporary pleasure that not adhering to the precepts allows them. I am speaking about, say, the hardworking low-wage worker who takes their kids to McDonald's for hamburgers, a meal that is within their financial means. Such a person is balancing lots of things: their financial constraints, their relationship with their children, their personal awareness of the impact of the fast-food industry on society at large, their own diet of ultra-processed food or fast food, and much more. Within this complex interplay of political, social, and personal dynamics, many of us are attached to our lifestyles even at a high cost to ourselves, those we love, and the world around us. Even Thầy has said that no one can practice the precepts perfectly, including the Buddha. Instead, Thầy says we need to live in such a way that we become aware of the suffering our actions perpetuate, make an effort to eradicate damage, and find wholesome, spiritual nourishment not only for ourselves but also for our children and future generations.[8]

Thầy has also said that we need to identify and recognize toxins already within us because the quality of our life depends, in part, on the amount of peace and joy within our body and our consciousness and how we share that peace and joy with others. The precepts support our well-being, protecting us individually and collectively from harm. Societal change happens at the roots by changing the individual and collective consciousness driven by greed, hatred, and delusion.[9]

The precepts are an invitation to be in touch with what is wholesome and beneficial in and around us. They are bells of mindfulness. Ultimately, the precepts are opportunities to live and grow a compassionate life of love, peace, and understanding. We might be challenged in our practice at times, and at those times we need to recommit ourselves and reconnect with spiritual friends who support us on the path toward living a healthy and wholesome life.

The precepts are part of a set of interconnected teachings that include the Noble Eightfold Path, the Four Noble Truths, and the Five Spiritual Powers: faith, diligence, mindfulness, concentration, and insight. These powers are interconnected in that faith leads to diligence, diligence leads to mindfulness, and the power of mindfulness fosters concentration, which gives rise to insight. Thầy has said that each of us needs to have our own experience of the precepts to fully understand them. Thầy advises us not to be caught in the "outer form" of practicing with the precepts. It can be counterproductive to follow the precepts as rigid dos and don'ts, or "rules," without understanding their deeper significance. An example from my own life was when I was caught in the form of speaking truthfully. I held rigidly to the precept around speaking honestly even when doing so was harmful to me and did not support the other person.

Thầy says that we should recognize three dimensions of the Trainings, which add depth and substance to our practice of mindfulness. The first dimension is *samvara sila*, or refraining from negative action. In body, speech, and mind, we need to refrain from harmful conduct. The second dimension is *kushaladharma sila*, engaging in positive action. When we see someone who needs our help, and we have the ability to reach out to help but we don't do it, this is a breach of the precept, according to Thầy. He says, "We have to do what is needed to be done.... When you see something happening that should not be happening, something unjust, then you have to intervene."[10] The third dimension is *sattvarthakriya sila*. According to this aspect of *sila*, even when there is no urgent situation where we need to intervene, we must continue to cultivate a compassionate heart and mind. This is the *bodhisattva* path of awakened action of service and love.

The precepts are not about telling us what to do and what not to do. They are about refraining from unwholesome action, performing wholesome action, and supporting all living beings, creating a better world for all.

I received the Five Mindfulness Trainings in 1998 and the Fourteen Mindfulness Trainings in 2003. I came to rely on all the Trainings during a period of profound turmoil in my life that began around 2015. I had a nagging sense, which I couldn't shake, that my life was going to become very complicated, and I was right. At the time, I was in a sad and unfulfilling marriage, and my career as a lawyer-lobbyist consumed every ounce of my life energy. The troubles began in 2016 with my father's long illness leading up to his death, which was followed by my brother Elliot's heart transplant in 2017; the end of my marriage in 2019; the death of my oldest brother,

Sam, in February 2020; the death of his wife, Dolores, in July 2020; the destruction of my house by Hurricane Ida in September 2021; the death of my youngest brother, Charles, in April 2022; and to add to all this, the COVID-19 pandemic and Black Lives Matter movement that ensued. These crushing losses and social and political upheavals within the United States and worldwide literally rearranged my sense of self, my sense of inner equilibrium, and how I viewed the world.

Here's how the unraveling of my life began, and how the precepts supported me. In 2016, I was on my way to London to offer teachings at Woodbrooke, a Quaker retreat and study center outside the city. The moment I stepped on the flight, my phone rang. It was my brother Elliot, who said, "Dad's not doing well."

"But I literally just stepped on the flight to London," I said. "Please let me know how he's doing when I get off the flight." My heart sank and my stomach churned all the way to London.

At best, I had a tumultuous relationship with my father. When I was a very small child, he abandoned the family, literally walked out, not to be seen again for years. My mother died when I was sixteen from overwork—she supported four children, working two jobs as a maid and a barber. After a turn of circumstances, my father decided to return to "be a dad." But that didn't work out, so I split at age eighteen with only some of my belongings in a sheet. I didn't see or speak to him for many years. However, after my first divorce, I realized that my father might have something to do with why my marriage had failed and why I found it so difficult to feel anything other than rage. I wrote him a letter and asked if I could come and visit him. He agreed. After a few days with him, I asked him *the* questions that lay like a steel plate on my heart: *Why did you treat me the way you did? Why did you beat me up? Why did you walk out on us?*

I will never forget his reply. He said plainly, truthfully, almost innocently, "I did the best I could."

At that moment, I felt an electric charge in my body and a flash of recognition. I knew what he said was true; his reality was just that. He did the best he could, the best he knew. Going forward in my life would mean healing from and transforming the brutality he inherited and passed on to me.

My dad, a cruel and hardened Jamaican, had been neglected, abused, beaten, and abandoned as a child. As I watched him age into his nineties, he became a very different person. Amazingly, he softened. I got a glimpse of who he was before he suffered neglect and abuse.

My father and I were able to find ways to connect and show our care for each other. That's why I left everything when another call came from my brother Elliot. I had been at Woodbrooke for about a week. I dropped my obligations to teach and my plans to visit the Lake District, and I boarded the next flight.

When I arrived at my dad's home in Florida, the hospital bed was in the middle of the living room, and there were people gathering and milling about. I gently held his hand and said, "I'm here, Dad, it's Valerie. I love you." There was a moment of recognition on his face and then nothing. He took his last breath while I held his hand. His life story was complete and the life lesson for me had just begun.

There were endless moments of grief and loss that shaped my life after my father died in 2016, and after Elliot's heart transplant in 2017. As one life loss snowballed into the next, I felt numb; the blur of losses did not give me a chance to grieve even the first loss. In my family, I was seen as "the strong one," the person who had it all together, the successful lawyer-lobbyist who would come in, take charge, make things happen, and make decisions others could not or would not. I was so overcome that I was totally unaware of the looming global COVID-19 pandemic as another turning point happened: the death of my oldest brother, Sam, in February 2020.

At 2 a.m., I arrived by Sam's bedside. The nurse on call said he had "taken a turn for the worse." He had stopped breathing; his heart was giving out. There was nothing more they could do. Lying there, he looked so peaceful, so quiet. I sat beside him, the two of us together in the darkness and stillness.

When someone you love dies, it's like standing frozen between moments. You're swept away on a wave of grief, without a handhold, in freefall. Your feet never touch solid ground, and instead you find yourself being pulled farther out from shore, down, down, down. Your world shatters and your heart aches, empty with unbearable darkness and heaviness.

I loved my oldest brother Sam in ways that I could only fully understand *after* he died. There was never a time when he wasn't there; he was a constant in my life. He knew all my shadows and secrets, the disgraces and bitter pills of life that I consumed. I could hide nothing from Sam—and I didn't want to. We laughed together, cried together, danced together, and complained about all the sucky things of life together, and he taught me about a particular kind of grace that is undefended and openhearted.

Sam was the person who brought me to the path of mindfulness practice in the Plum Village tradition. The year was 1995, and I was sitting in Sam's Upper West Side apartment when he opened *The New York Times*. There was an image of Thích Nhất Hạnh, who was offering a talk just down the street at the Riverside Church. Sam knew nothing about Buddhism. He knew nothing about Thích Nhất Hạnh. But he knew a lot about me. At the time, I was deeply ensconced in my big, demanding job as a lawyer-lobbyist. I was Type A, hard as nails, hypercritical, full of tension and stress, rageful, and quick tempered. Knowing all this, Sam casually said, "Just go on down there and listen to that guy." Because Sam was always right, I did.

Four or five hours later, I walked out of the church, shaking my head and saying to myself, "Oh no, that's not for me." Thầy had talked about finding peace and compassion within and sharing it with others. He described breathing as an act of conscious awareness, of love. A part of me thought, "If I believe Thầy's words, what would that say about the legal career that I oh-so-carefully crafted, the sacrifice, the backbreaking effort to make myself into something respectable?" Another part of me instantly knew Thầy offered me a path that I could never have imagined. That path included a radical shift in mindset of what "career" means, of how to integrate suffering, and of what it means to be a "somebody."

Sam is gone from this physical plane, from the historical dimension of his selfhood. Yet he is with me every day in the ultimate dimension of self where there is no birth, no death, no after, no before. I am not saying that Sam's death wasn't a crushing blow and didn't rearrange my worldview. It did. I am saying that I hold the reality of his physical death *and* understand that his life and our relationship led me to something other than his death and my feelings of loss and despair. His death led me to accept and appreciate the tenderness of this very moment, which is filled with both potential and pain, beauty and destruction, and to realize that when I look at my hand, I can see Sam's manifestation right here in me. Paradoxically, I miss him greatly, and yet I also feel deeply connected to him. Sam is in me and with me, and I am with him.

Sam's death was a continuation of a series of losses that grabbed me by the throat, consumed all my waking hours, and followed me into sleep. All of those losses—my father's death, the end of my marriage, my brother Elliot's agonizing heart transplant, Sam's death and the death of his beloved wife, the devastation of Hurricane Ida, the death of my youngest brother, Charles—left me broken into many pieces without time or space to recover. I kept "soldiering on" from one loss to the next. In the midst of all of this, in 2018 I received Lamp Transmission to become a Dharma teacher in the Plum Village tradition. So much was happening all at once that I could hardly take in what this meant for me. What I did know was that I had transformed enormous suffering, and others witnessed this transformation. I did know that I had inner guidance to help me through this time and that the precepts were part of this inner guidance system. Over time, I came to reflect on what it means to engage the precepts as a means of guidance for the losses and for the loves of my life. Only recently did I understand what research validates: People from marginalized communities experience higher incidents of prolonged grief disorder, sometimes cited as complicated or compound grief that is exacerbated by factors such as race and gender.

–

Marisela:

At times when we feel our ground shifting under us, our world changing faster than we can keep up, and the ethics of our environment challenged, we turn inward to understand. We also search the shelves, the computer, and the Internet for "that" teaching, "that" phrase, "that" song, "that" reminder of "that" truth we hold dear. We look for our guiding light, the solidity that reaffirms our values, and ask ourselves, "How are we to act in these changing and chaotic times?"

This was the context as we neared mid-May 2020. COVID-19 was raging its war against humans across the world; we were isolated from our social networks, our work relationships, and our schedules of—more or less—choice. It was a pandemic and we were told that social distancing was the only way to prevent becoming infected and maybe dying. People we knew were becoming infected one day and dying a week later. Black and Brown bodies, bodies in the service industry, bodies considered dispensable, bodies working for low-income wages were again the ones at the front lines, being infected and dying. We did not know what to do.

Then on May 25, 2020, another video went viral, highlighting unlawful police violence against a Black man. In Minneapolis,

Minnesota, George Floyd was accused by a store clerk of paying with a counterfeit bill, and was approached by the police. Shortly thereafter one of the officers kneeled on his neck while two others stood nearby and a crowd of spectators watched. The officer kneeled on his neck for more than nine minutes, listening to Floyd pleading that he could not breathe, until he died. This one act of violence against a Black man was videotaped, shared, and broadcast over and over on the news, so we collectively lived through another heartbreaking event of militarized violence. Some of us felt it in our bodies, in our hearts, in our DNA, in our ancestors. And we were traumatized again. The ground under us continued to shift. We were angry, sick, heartbroken, and confused again. Many of us turned to our inner ethical guidelines for living a life of value and to figure out what to do. Because the United States was in a lockdown to support social distancing and prevent new COVID-19 infections, we felt extraordinarily isolated at a time when we needed each other most. There were protests and rallies as the Black Lives Matter movement organized across the US to question and bring attention to the militarized policing that continued to target systemically marginalized peoples. This movement spread across Canada and other countries. We felt chaos and confusion in the collective consciousness, and we felt, as Black and Brown bodies, hated.

I wanted to be on the streets but was too weak to be there. I had contracted COVID-19 and had been very sick since February 2020. I was evaluated in the ER with many tests and still had no diagnosis because we didn't know much about COVID-19 at that time. I couldn't walk and could only stand for a few minutes before having to lie down. There were body pains spreading, night sweats and fevers, headaches, chest pains, and severe fatigue and weakness, and no test could account for a cause. Against doctor's orders I chose to go home instead of being hospitalized for more tests, and there I stayed for several months. My medicine was rest, prayer, and a very high dose of a steroid. Like animals who remain still under a tree when they are ill, I moved from the couch to the bed and back for two months, relying on the kindness of friends to bring me food and care. During this time, not knowing when there would be changes in my body led me to think I was going to transition. One night in the midst of body sweat and tremors, I came to peace with that happening. I vividly remember my feeling of regret that I didn't have the energy to organize the closet and felt sorry for the person who would have to sort through it. This feeling underscored the social conditioning of female-bodied people in our role as caretakers and cleaners. Things changed, as they always do. I began feeling stronger, experiencing less body pain, and feeling less confused and more clearheaded. By early May, I slowly began walking outside again, initially for three minutes at a time, then daily increasing my capacity.

In May, my dear friend Valerie and I began discussing the impact of the death of George Floyd and the COVID-19 pandemic on us, the pain and isolation many of us were experiencing, and our own personal suffering in these moments. While we were practicing with our ethical guidelines for a truthful and skillful life—the Five Mindfulness Trainings of the Plum Village Community of Engaged Buddhism—we felt that it was critical to name the suffering occurring in the moment. We were looking for teachings that would help us live this specific moment with compassion instead of anger, and keep our hearts open instead of closing them. While the Five Mindfulness Trainings (referred to at times as the Trainings, guidelines, or precepts) offered us comfort and direction, we knew that other people in marginalized groups were also seeking to see this moment directly in the Trainings. We decided to comment on the existing Five Mindfulness Trainings by applying them explicitly to the experience of many marginalized groups. This resulted in the co-creation of the Contemplations on the Five Mindfulness Trainings (referred to at times as simply the Contemplations, a commentary on the Trainings).

The Contemplations lift up into words the racism and social injustices of this moment and the history leading up to it, naming these collective sufferings explicitly. They invite us to look deeper into the Trainings, to assure a future of compassion and understanding can evolve for our descendants—and our ancestors who directly and indirectly suffered from these injustices. The Contemplations do not name everyone's experiences because we do not know the suffering of all people. What we know, though, is that the suffering of the Black body is interconnected with the suffering of the Asian body and all bodies. We know that police violence is enacted against many groups of people, and that violence is enacted not only by the police but by people in our own tribes and families and also by ourselves against ourselves. **We invite the reader to reflect on the interbeing nature of all suffering and all joy. Can we see the suffering of the other as our own suffering?**

The teachings on nonduality offered by Buddhism help us to see how "othering" is the path of suffering. As long as we separate ourselves from each other and find ways to keep these fabricated separations as a reality, we continue to produce structures and systems that easily justify the rights of one group over another. We build up our individual and group identities relative to other individuals or groups. We compare ourselves to others and blame them for our suffering. We look for differences instead of similarities.

Thầy teaches us that when we can see the interconnected nature of all things, we begin to let go of the illusion of separation, of the duality of being and nonbeing.[11] We then extinguish the fire that feeds this delusion and become free of dualistic notions. We can experience a unity that liberates us from the suffering of separation. When we can let go of this illusion of a separate self, or a supposed true self, then we realize that we are actually conditioned by many things: our parents, our environments, our political ecosystems, and the many people and their experiences and their ideas that have landed in us and that we have consumed. We are conditioned by each other.[12]

The invitation is to look into our perceptions of similarity and difference and to offer compassion for ourselves as well as others who are living a different set of life experiences. Can we experience the joy of someone who is different from us? This is the practice of sympathetic joy, happiness for others, which helps us to cultivate a mind of kindness and openness. In Buddhism, sympathetic joy and compassion are two of the states of mind we train ourselves to practice, called the Four Immeasurables, the Divine Abodes, or *brahmaviharas*—the dwelling places of enlightened ones. The more we train our mind to dwell in compassion and sympathetic joy, the more likely we are to experience a balanced heart that can stay the course of kindness and inclusivity (the other two divine abodes). We train in this way to realize the interbeing (interconnected) nature of ourselves with others and emerge from our delusions of superiority, inferiority, and equality.[13] We begin to understand that we are not separate from one another because we are made up of the same things: parents, ancestors, experiences, societal and cultural norms, and the elements of earth, water, wind, and sun. Like all living beings, we would not exist if even one of these different elements were removed.

This understanding that we are not separate, that there really is no "other" person, that we are interconnected, is our path toward waking up and staying awake. This path is simple, and yet it's difficult to keep living it each day. We need help to stay on the path; we need signs or guides. The yellow or red signs called blazes that we find on the hiking trails can be likened to the Five Mindfulness Trainings. Blazes help us stay on the path we begin at the trailhead. Without them, we might lose our way. In a world filled with distractions, we can remember the path we set out on, the path of liberation, the path of true love and understanding, by remembering the Trainings and practicing them, contemplating and reflecting until they become part of our lives. Thầy encouraged us to read them at regular intervals and reflect on how we might have studied and practiced with them in daily life. At times, we might have a teacher or friend on the path who reminds us to stay on it. This person is a trailblazer for us, like the people who put signs on trees to help us follow the trail. They become our sign, our guide, our spiritual friend, to keep us on this path of liberation.

The Five Mindfulness Trainings

The Five Mindfulness Trainings represent the Buddhist vision for a global spirituality and ethic. They are a concrete expression of the Buddha's teachings on the Four Noble Truths and the Noble Eightfold Path, the path of right understanding and true love, leading to healing, transformation, and happiness for ourselves and for the world. To practice the Five Mindfulness Trainings is to cultivate the insight of interbeing, or Right View, which can remove all discrimination, intolerance, anger, fear, and despair. If we live according to the Five Mindfulness Trainings, we are already on the path of a bodhisattva. Knowing we are on that path, we are not lost in confusion about our life in the present or in fears about the future.

Reverence for Life

Aware of the suffering caused by the destruction of life, I am committed to cultivating the insight of interbeing and compassion and learning ways to protect the lives of people, animals, plants, and minerals. I am determined not to kill, not to let others kill, and not to support any act of killing in the world, in my thinking, or in my way of life. Seeing that harmful actions arise from anger, fear, greed, and intolerance, which in turn come from dualistic and discriminative thinking, I will cultivate openness, non-discrimination, and non-attachment to views in order to transform violence, fanaticism, and dogmatism in myself and in the world.

True Happiness

Aware of the suffering caused by exploitation, social injustice, stealing, and oppression, I am committed to practicing generosity in my thinking, speaking, and acting. I am determined not to steal and not to possess anything that should belong to others; and I will share my time, energy, and material resources with those who are in need. I will practice looking deeply to see that the happiness and suffering of others are not separate from my own happiness and suffering; that true happiness is not possible without understanding and compassion; and that running after wealth, fame, power and sensual pleasures can bring much suffering and despair. I am aware that happiness depends on my mental attitude and not on external conditions, and that I can live happily in the present moment simply by remembering that I already have more than enough conditions to be happy. I am committed to practicing Right Livelihood so that I can help reduce the suffering of living beings on earth and stop contributing to climate change.

True Love

Aware of the suffering caused by sexual misconduct, I am committed to cultivating responsibility and learning ways to protect the safety and integrity of individuals, couples, families, and society. Knowing that sexual desire is not love, and that sexual activity motivated by craving always harms myself as well as others, I am determined not to engage in sexual relations without mutual consent, true love, and a deep, long-term commitment. I resolve to find spiritual support for the integrity of my relationship from family members, friends, and sangha with whom there is support and trust. I will do everything in my power to protect children from sexual abuse and to prevent couples and families from being broken by sexual misconduct. Seeing that body and mind are interrelated, I am committed to learn appropriate ways to take care of my sexual energy and to cultivate the four basic elements of true love—loving kindness, compassion, joy, and inclusiveness—for the greater happiness of myself and others. Recognizing the diversity of human experience, I am committed not to discriminate against any form of gender identity or sexual orientation. Practicing true love, we know that we will continue beautifully into the future.

Loving Speech and Deep Listening

Aware of the suffering caused by unmindful speech and the inability to listen to others, I am committed to cultivating loving speech and compassionate listening in order to relieve suffering and to promote reconciliation and peace in myself and among other people, ethnic and religious groups, and nations. Knowing that words can create happiness or suffering, I am committed to speaking truthfully using words that inspire confidence, joy, and hope. When anger is manifesting in me, I am determined not to speak. I will practice mindful breathing and walking in order to recognize and to look deeply into my anger. I know that the roots of anger can be found in my wrong perceptions and lack of understanding of the suffering in myself and in the other person. I will speak and listen in a way that can help myself and the other person to transform suffering and see the way out of difficult situations. I am determined not to spread news that I do not know to be certain and not to utter words that can cause division or discord. I will practice Right Diligence to nourish my capacity for understanding, love, joy, and inclusiveness, and gradually transform anger, violence, and fear that lie deep in my consciousness.

Nourishment and Healing

Aware of the suffering caused by unmindful consumption, I am committed to cultivating good health, both physical and mental, for myself, my family, and my society by practicing mindful eating, drinking, and consuming. I will practice looking deeply into how I consume the Four Kinds of Nutriments, namely edible foods, sense impressions, volition, and consciousness. I am determined not to gamble, or to use alcohol, drugs, or any other products which contain toxins, such as certain websites, electronic games, TV programs, films, magazines, books, and conversations. I will practice coming back to the present moment to be in touch with the refreshing, healing, and nourishing elements in me and around me, not letting regrets and sorrow drag me back into the past nor letting anxieties, fear, or craving pull me out of the present moment. I am determined not to try to cover up loneliness, anxiety, or other suffering by losing myself in consumption. I will contemplate interbeing and consume in a way that preserves peace, joy, and well-being in my body and consciousness, and in the collective body and consciousness of my family, my society, and the earth.[14]

2

Living into the Five Mindfulness Trainings

Along with other Buddhist teachings, the Trainings offer guidance on how to handle everyday life situations—how to act and how not to act to increase our happiness and decrease our suffering. They are not separate from daily life but are woven into our awareness about the choices we make. In this section, we take turns to discuss our personal approaches to exploring and understanding these precepts. We share a few instances of how the Trainings have shaped our lives and kept us steady on this path of love as liberation from separation, violence, and unkindness.

Marisela:

When I first read the Five Mindfulness Trainings, I thought, "This is the same as what my grandmother taught me." Accepting the Trainings felt like coming back home. They immediately made sense intellectually, and even more importantly, my body felt at ease, rooted, and reconnected to my grandmother's wisdom.

The First Mindfulness Training

Reverence for Life

Aware of the suffering caused by the destruction of life, I am committed to cultivating the insight of interbeing and compassion and learning ways to protect the lives of people, animals, plants, and minerals. I am determined not to kill, not to let others kill, and not to support any act of killing in the world, in my thinking, or in my way of life. Seeing that harmful actions arise from anger, fear, greed, and intolerance, which in turn come from dualistic and discriminative thinking, I will cultivate openness, non-discrimination, and non-attachment to views in order to transform violence, fanaticism, and dogmatism in myself and in the world.

Valerie:

I came into a deeper understanding of the First Mindfulness Training as a result of my relationship with my brother Sam. Perhaps more than anyone else, he taught me the enduring and boundless capacity of love. He taught me to allow myself to find love in quite unexpected places, especially in preparing a meal as love and in the food I consumed. In those days, I was a militant vegetarian, meaning I had a bad attitude. I felt superior to others about my diet because I was not consuming meat. Every time I went over to the Upper West Side apartment of Sam and his wife, Dolores, Sam did all the cooking and he loved every moment. The kitchen was his forest refuge, the place that brought him joy and happiness, and it showed in the sumptuous meals he prepared. His "church" was sharing his cooking with others. He spent hours perfecting his signature dishes: curry chicken, oxtail, or crispy fried Jamaican Escovitch fish. Although I could smell the curry and tamarind when I got off the elevator, I would have none of it in my righteousness.

It was Thanksgiving, and Sam spent hours making a Jamaican feast of curry chicken, pork loin, collards soaked in ham hocks, corn bread loaded with butter, and more. I had just finished reading Thích Nhất Hạnh's book on food as an expression of love. I realized this dinner wasn't a meal—it was Sam's way of expressing love. Just then, I turned to Sam and said, "I'll have everything." He looked at me, shocked, and then joy slowly spread across his face with a mile-wide grin, revealing the gap between his two front teeth. I ate it all, and with every mouthful I savored his love. He was the happiest I had ever seen him, and so was I.

In this case, the compassionate and virtuous action was to consume meat as an expression of love and respect for my brother. Right Action is to understand that the basis for the First Precept is non-harming, and in that moment, the best way I could demonstrate non-harming was through eating the food my brother graciously and joyfully served me. Right Action was to meet Sam on his own terms and to be flexible and nondogmatic in my views. My wider values around the ecological impact of meat consumption, including its effects on the environment and on the animals themselves, has not changed. How we approach each precept isn't one-size-fits-all but invites a deeper look.

Marisela:

The First Mindfulness Training, Reverence for Life, invites us to remember the preciousness of *all* life forms and to be in awareness of the suffering that occurs when we do not remember. One memorable insight from practicing this Training was recognizing that I was socialized not to have reverence for *myself*. As a Black-Brown female-bodied person who immigrated to the United States at the age of thirteen, I quickly recognized that these group identities were marginalized and considered inferior in the dualistic scheme of the worth of a life: male versus female, white versus person of color, US-born versus immigrant, low income versus wealthy. Male, white, US-born, and wealthy are all deemed superior to female, person of color, immigrant, and low income. Through the first Training, my realization that all lives should be revered and loved has shifted my love and respect for myself and for others in various marginalized groups whose lives have been devalued in society, at times leading to their deaths. This Training has also helped me name why we must cultivate inclusive spiritual sanctuaries that invite in all our diverse forms to be present. This assures that not just some folks will find their freedom individually, but that *all* folks will find their liberation collectively. In white-majority spaces like many of the Buddhist spaces in North America, this Training helped me name out loud when there were minimal or no other BIPOC folks in the space. This naming came from a fierce understanding that all our lives are worthy of reverence, not just some, and therefore we all need to be on this path of liberation. My path, before engaging with the teachings of Thầy and other Buddhist teachers, always involved critiquing the lack of BIPOC people, female-identified bodies, low-income people, and other marginalized people in the various spaces I moved through. Sometimes this critique would be pointed and sharp, and at times it would not land for others and therefore not effect beneficial change.

With my understanding of this Training, and a self-embracing of my own reverence in this form, truly feeling sufficient as I am, my critique continues. This critique is now more powerful because it does not come from a place of feeling diminished or inferior; it comes from a clear understanding that we are all interconnected, and that the dualism of superiority and inferiority is false and irreverent. It's not only false and irreverent in the mundane realm; it is also false and irreverent in the absolute realm. Our Buddha nature—who we really are—is nondiscriminating, and therefore we all have the potential to become enlightened. I continue to speak up and invite those around me to remember that their inferiority complex rests on the dualistic notion that groups with little or no socially constructed power are somehow diminished in their Buddha nature. And I remind those with a superiority complex, also constructed through social norms, that their perceptions are also false because we all have Buddha nature, and waking up from the delusion of our separation is our collective journey of awakening. No one group has the enlightenment "gene" predetermined. However, we can all acknowledge that some groups with more privileged circumstances, cultivated through unfair social norms, have more conditions at their disposal for practicing on this path of awakening. This is why we must build more inclusive sacred spaces through financial support for those in need. We can do this throughout the larger society by providing more fair and equitable access to education, housing, health, recreation, and employment so everyone who chooses to attend retreats and take time to rest, care for themselves, and study and practice the teachings of awakening and love can do so.

The Second Mindfulness Training

True Happiness

Aware of the suffering caused by exploitation, social injustice, stealing, and oppression, I am committed to practicing generosity in my thinking, speaking, and acting. I am determined not to steal and not to possess anything that should belong to others; and I will share my time, energy, and material resources with those who are in need. I will practice looking deeply to see that the happiness and suffering of others are not separate from my own happiness and suffering; that true happiness is not possible without understanding and compassion; and that running after wealth, fame, power and sensual pleasures can bring much suffering and despair. I am aware that happiness depends on my mental attitude and not on external conditions, and that I can live happily in the present moment simply by remembering that I already have more than enough conditions to be happy. I am committed to practicing Right Livelihood so that I can help reduce the suffering of living beings on earth and stop contributing to climate change.

Valerie:

For me, this Training is not only about not taking things that don't belong to me. It is also about not infringing on people's time, or "stealing" it, in ways that fail to recognize that their life energy is a precious and nonrenewable resource. This Training is closely related to the path of Right Livelihood and voluntary simplicity because it reminds us to engage in work that supports rather than destroys life. It is about understanding that structural inequities in society perpetuate systems that oppress the most vulnerable people and beings on earth, while also encouraging economic models and forms of government that support individual and collective overuse of earth's resources.

My understanding of this precept grew over many years. I attended Howard School of Law, a historically Black college, at the time of the great Civil Rights leaders. These leaders were frequent visitors at the school, including Mrs. Rosa Parks, Andrew Young, James Baldwin, and the person I most admired, Justice Thurgood Marshall. As young law students, we adored Marshall. He was a grandfatherly figure to us, and of course we were intimately familiar with his landmark decision, Brown v. Board of Education. Marshall helped to author and argue this historic decision, which desegregated public schools in the United States in 1954. Each time Marshall came to the school and gathered with us, he began by asking one important question: "What is the quality of your intention?" He did *not* ask what our intention was. At first, I didn't fully understand what he was getting at. As a law student at Howard, I studied the history of legally sanctioned inequities, injustice, discrimination, and oppression. I came to understand that the energy and mindset behind intentions were of equal importance with the very intention we cultivate. Marshall was encouraging us to see the bigger picture as we sought justice, to understand what drives inequities, and to understand harm that can arise from laws crafted without regard for the most disenfranchised. I began to understand that happiness is closely linked to a moral quality of service in support of a better society, and that this service arises from our deepest aspirations to create a better world.

Marisela:

The Second Mindfulness Training, True Happiness, continues to support my practice of living simply. Living a simple life requires the spiritual friend of the mindfulness trainings to continuously remind me how my choices directly or indirectly contribute to social injustice. For example, if I continue to spend my dollars at Amazon (the world's largest online retailer and one of the top five multinational tech companies), I am directly contributing to wealth accumulation in the hands of a monopoly that does not pay a living wage to its employees and does not support inclusivity in its workforce. The company and its leadership seek ongoing wealth accumulation by extracting, or stealing, time and energy from workers, and do not practice wealth redistribution through fair wages.[15]

This Training also helped me view how the effects of extraction, exploitation, stealing, and taking the life energy of people lead to the manifestation of seeds of fear, anger, and other similar emotions. This Training reminds me that with awareness, I can generate the seed of mindfulness to manifest right alongside my anger, my rage, my hatred. Mindfulness can help me understand and be in relationship with these seeds and keep me from harming myself and others. When we practice with mindfulness, we bring its energy to be present with our fear and other mental formations that are triggered by the greed and hatred we experience and see around us. All these mental formations, energetic formations, or seeds, are in us. With Right Effort and Right Mindfulness, two elements of the Noble Eightfold Path, we notice what is arising and decide what to do to take care of the mental formations.

I can see how to take good care of my anger by acknowledging and engaging with the anger. I do not push it away or punish myself for being angry. I simply shine light on it by naming it for what it is, understand why it is here with me, and figure out how to transform it. Sometimes I have to do this over and over again. For example, when the 47th president of the United States turns a blind eye to the violence occurring in countries like Palestine, Ukraine, Haiti, Cuba, Sudan, and others, or denies the effect of climate change on our most vulnerable countries, anger can rise up in me. Immediately, rising right alongside my anger, my mindfulness keeps an eye on my anger. The conversation may go something like this: "Hello, old friend, I see you. Here we are again. Let us acknowledge why we are here again." This type of engagement is healthy and transformative. Mindfulness is a good friend that I want to stay around a long time. During these times of heightened fear and anger due to an unchecked, growing authoritarian regime in the United States, a new norm is allowing widespread greed, hatred, and delusion to persist, and is bringing many atrocities to our most marginalized populations. This second Training allows happiness to be present right alongside the anger and fear resulting from these triggers. True happiness does not have to be absent of fear or worry. No, mindfulness allows them to coexist and prevents them from causing harm.

My anger shows up in my body and alerts me that something is not right. This anger can motivate me to act, and to practice more, because as I see more moments of anger arising, I want to make sure I cultivate the mind and heart that assure mindfulness will continue to co-arise with my anger. I do not let my anger stay alone because in the past, my unattended anger and fear led to actions that I later regretted. This looked like me feeling justified for causing harm to someone through harsh speech in retaliation because they had caused harm through violent speech. This Training helped my lifelong path of social justice become compassionate and less harmful by revealing the nonduality beyond good and bad. In the midst of anger, being able to give rise to another energy—like mindfulness, or patience, or deep looking—to take care of the anger, already removes its power to alone rule my mind. When I remember to practice in this way, I can now take good care of all the seeds that arise in my mind, with Right Action and without judgment. When I allow anger to take over, letting this seed grow larger, my mind becomes clouded by one mental formation. There is a cycle of consuming anger and being consumed by anger. I am clear that being motivated by anger is not how I want to exist in the world. What I prefer is to not judge myself when anger arises, to take care of this anger, and to respond to the injustices leading to my anger from a place of deep looking, clarity, and open-mindedness. This way of responsiveness leads me to happiness. I can let anger be my path of compassion and insight.

The Third Mindfulness Training

True Love

Aware of the suffering caused by sexual misconduct, I am committed to cultivating responsibility and learning ways to protect the safety and integrity of individuals, couples, families, and society. Knowing that sexual desire is not love, and that sexual activity motivated by craving always harms myself as well as others, I am determined not to engage in sexual relations without mutual consent, true love, and a deep, long-term commitment. I resolve to find spiritual support for the integrity of my relationship from family members, friends, and sangha with whom there is support and trust. I will do everything in my power to protect children from sexual abuse and to prevent couples and families from being broken by sexual misconduct. Seeing that body and mind are interrelated, I am committed to learn appropriate ways to take care of my sexual energy and to cultivate the four basic elements of true love—loving kindness, compassion, joy, and inclusiveness—for the greater happiness of myself and others. Recognizing the diversity of human experience, I am committed not to discriminate against any form of gender identity or sexual orientation. Practicing true love, we know that we will continue beautifully into the future.

Valerie:

This Training, or precept, invites us to examine on an individual level how we engage our sexual energies. On a societal level, it asks us to reflect on the capitalist, patriarchal, misogynistic, and white supremacist systems and structures that promote male dominance and exploitation of women, and that perpetuate violence, hatred, greed, and delusion. The precept also asks us to consider the ways that socially constructed norms of masculinity and femininity impact how we think about our own and others' identities, and how these norms shape our ways of thinking and relating to others and to ourselves.

I came to my personal understanding of this precept years ago, after a failed and frustrating relationship with Jimmy, a man I dated and fell head over heels in love with. I was still getting over my first divorce and feeling desperate to fill the void with a meaningful relationship. I met him through a personal ad, the precursor of today's online dating, in a local magazine. His written description checked so many of my boxes that I was immediately drawn to him. We agreed to meet at my favorite coffee shop in Old City, Philadelphia. When he arrived, he brought a gift of a book by Peace Pilgrim, an American spiritual teacher, mystic, vegetarian, and peace activist who in 1952 became the first woman to walk the entire length of the Appalachian Trail (2,197.4 miles) in one season. Unbeknownst to Jimmy, I had newly discovered Peace Pilgrim's writings and had become totally consumed in learning more about her life. When he walked into the coffee shop with her book, I could hardly believe it.

The relationship moved fast and furiously. Jimmy was seductive, charming, and charismatic. He was a Quaker who understood Buddhism, an avid gardener and hiker, smart and witty, funny and emotional. We talked for hours about forgiveness and Christology. I was totally undefended and became like clay in his hands. I so wanted a loving relationship, to be cherished, to be seen, heard, and understood. I became sexually intimate with him way too fast and too soon, and shortly after we became intimate, he dumped me. He didn't return my phone calls; he suddenly became unavailable. It took months for me to get over this bitter pill. I felt used, and even worse, humiliated and disappointed in myself for not seeing all this coming, not having better judgment. And then, just when I regained my equilibrium, Jimmy called out of the clear blue, wanting to know how I was doing and if we could meet up for coffee. Because I still had feelings for him, I said, "Yes." Shortly thereafter, we became intimate again, and you guessed it, he dumped me again—disappeared, didn't call. Again, I fell into a deep depression, berating myself for having poor judgment, for being a sucker. Again, it took months to get over the hurt and disappointment, but time heals, and eventually, I did.

Months later, I was sitting in my office in the middle of a sunny day when the phone rang. It was Jimmy. He said he wanted to be respectful of me. He said he was not sure what to do and that he wanted to see me again. He asked me, "What should *I* do?" With great clarity and self-esteem, I said, "Well, Jimmy, I'm not sure what *you* should do, but I do know what *I* should do: I really have no idea of what's going on with you and I hope you find out soon before you do to others what you did to me. I have no interest in keeping whatever this is going any further. The kindest, clearest thing I can say is, I no longer want any contact with you." I hung up the phone and went on with my day feeling somewhat vindicated, but more importantly feeling that I was on my own side, that I could see clearly my own longing and delusion, and I sensed that his confusion need not be my confusion.

What did I learn about the Third Mindfulness Training from Jimmy? At that time, I had a fleeting awareness of this precept. I learned that I fell into the relationship because I was very needy—and that was okay. Acknowledging that we all have needs was actually a step up for me. For years, I walked around with the belief that I had no needs, that needs were for dependent, weak people, and I was the opposite: strong, independent, and self-sufficient. Of course, that belief system was formed and flourished as an adaptive response to a childhood of parental abandonment, death, poverty, abuse, and neglect. Decades later, by the time I connected to Jimmy, I was lonely after my divorce and I wanted to feel loved and cared for. I wanted Jimmy, somebody, anybody to love me in ways that only I could love myself but didn't know how. Today, I know that loving myself doesn't mean narcissism or self-inflation. It means being in relationship with myself, being in contact with my feelings, accepting and loving myself, appreciating all the aspects of me—especially the parts that are hyper-self-sufficient, independent, and need-denying. It means loving my body, mind, spirit, all the parts of me, the parts that I like and dislike, the shadow and the light. I know, too, that loving myself is offering unconditional love for myself in good times and in bad times, especially in hard times when I am feeling my insecurities, weaknesses, and flaws. Perhaps most of all, loving myself is about offering myself forgiveness and self-grace, being the first to be on my side, and being in active dialogue with myself when I am feeling lonely and hurt.

The Third Mindfulness Training has taught me that love and loneliness are very interconnected and that I cannot expect anyone to love me better or more than I love myself. My practice today is to cultivate an active, loving relationship with myself.

Marisela:

The Third Mindfulness Training, True Love, has provided a strong anchor for me in how I have engaged in sexual relations. The current form of this Training acknowledges the inclusivity of diverse gender and sexual relationships without heterosexism, thus inviting us all in as spiritual beings. This Training helped me look more deeply into the possibility of love without sexual relationships. It took some time and required me to choose to set aside sexual intimacy to discover what else was there. Like many, I had grown up understanding sexual relations as a natural, matter-of-fact way to engage with people instead of a loving way to engage with someone I trusted and who trusted me. Sexual relations had been an automatic outcome, almost an expectation, especially from male-bodied people. I appreciated the Training's invitation to reassess this expectation and consider choice in the matter of all sexual relations. As a child of sexual abuse, I am aware that this is a big deal for many of us: to be in choice after having it taken away at a young age. Sexual abuse at a young age can set us into habitual responses that become imprinted into our nervous system. I continue to unlearn this imprint and how it has conditioned me in all aspects of life.

Mindfulness has allowed me the space to learn how to notice my body's response in situations where a prelude to sexual intimacy might be the next step in a relationship. This space to notice is precious because I can begin to disentangle the effects of a lifetime of training and habit, and disentangle the body sensations from the heart sensations. For example, maybe the next step isn't sexual intimacy; maybe it's asking why I am feeling this type of desire now and what else is happening in this moment. This process has been revealing and has pointed to my habitual responses. It has been quite freeing. It also has allowed me to look at how true love can be defined outside of sexual intimacy. I continue to explore and live this Training by allowing spaciousness into any expectations held by me or others.

The Fourth Mindfulness Training

Loving Speech and Deep Listening

Aware of the suffering caused by unmindful speech and the inability to listen to others, I am committed to cultivating loving speech and compassionate listening in order to relieve suffering and to promote reconciliation and peace in myself and among other people, ethnic and religious groups, and nations. Knowing that words can create happiness or suffering, I am committed to speaking truthfully using words that inspire confidence, joy, and hope. When anger is manifesting in me, I am determined not to speak. I will practice mindful breathing and walking in order to recognize and to look deeply into my anger. I know that the roots of anger can be found in my wrong perceptions and lack of understanding of the suffering in myself and in the other person. I will speak and listen in a way that can help myself and the other person to transform suffering and see the way out of difficult situations. I am determined not to spread news that I do not know to be certain and not to utter words that can cause division or discord. I will practice Right Diligence to nourish my capacity for understanding, love, joy, and inclusiveness, and gradually transform anger, violence, and fear that lie deep in my consciousness.

Valerie:

This Training invites us to speak with honesty. It is closely related to the Noble Eightfold Path's Right Speech, which is considered truthful, useful, and kind, avoids gossip, and is generally constructive in nature. A common litmus test for truthful speech is to ask whether what you want to say is useful and timely, and whether it is yours to say or whether the words should come from someone else. This encompasses "speech" that happens between people in person and online, and includes social media, which is a primary vehicle for communication among many people.

I began practicing with this precept in work situations as a lawyer-lobbyist. When I first practiced mindfulness in the Plum Village tradition in the late 1990s, I was deeply consumed in my career, which meant I had little time for sitting meditation. At that time, practicing meditation as a lawyer and a lobbyist was unthinkable so I became a "closet meditator." Eventually, I decided to bring my meditation practice out of the closet and into the halls of Congress while I was actively engaged in lobbying. The job of a lobbyist is to convince people to do things that they otherwise wouldn't do, so

I spent a lot of time talking to people. I decided to actively practice mindfulness while I was speaking and listening to Democrats and Republicans whom I lobbied. In every conversation with a member of Congress, I began by feeling my feet on the floor and then the breath in my body. I paid close attention to any feelings and sensations: tightness, tension, anxiety, heaviness. I didn't open my mouth to say a word to the person I was lobbying until I genuinely felt calm and connected, free of tension in my body, with a sense of true care and sincere interest in them. I noticed that my speech changed. Because my body was free of tension and my mindset was one of genuine interest in the other person, my words were different. I said, "Tell me about how this affects you and your district." "I want to know, and I have time." "What do you think?" These open questions shifted the space between us. After asking these types of questions, I paused to listen with the sole purpose of understanding the other person. If I sensed struggle or agitation in the other person, I sought to listen as a way to offer relief to the other person. In turn, I noticed that with this way of speaking and listening people were less guarded and more open. I shifted from being a competent and expert lobbyist-lawyer to an emotional leader. My sense is that people perceived the emotional connection with myself and found that to be authentic and trustworthy, which supported our mutual relationship, mutual flourishing. Over many years of practicing in this way, my relationships shifted from seeking to influence and convince, a kind of power over, to a power with. My advocacy shifted. Eventually, other lobbyists and members of Congress began to say, "Gee, you don't seem like a lobbyist." Then I had to rediscover who I was and what I was meant to be.

This Training taught me the power of shifting my words from an effort to convince, persuade, and influence to an expression of care, kindness, and sincere interest in the other person. I learned to prioritize understanding over being right.

Marisela:

The Fourth Mindfulness Training, Loving Speech and Deep Listening, is probably my favorite Training. Once I was able to pause and practice deep listening, it was like a miracle. The profound shifts that occur from listening deeply to myself and another person are amazing. In a circle of people, I have experienced the power of collective deep listening to transform difficulties without using words. There is an energy that emerges when we fully focus on listening to others share from their hearts what is alive in that moment. This deep listening can occur inside us and outside of us. When a circle of people put aside their chattering mind and focus on the words of another, we offer a cradle of love and care. Through sharing their words, the person can rest in kindness and nonjudgment. I find listening to others similar to listening to myself during silent meditation. It's a turning toward what is coming up inside of me, meeting myself where I am and not turning away, whether the thoughts are difficult or joyful.

The practice of loving speech was and continues to be the Training that requires the most energy for me. In my experience, people who come from historically oppressed groups and those who have survived abusive conditions as young people consider part of our stepping into freedom the ability to speak our truth, finally. We have lived with generations of silence imposed on us, and finally we reach a place where we find our voices and want to exercise our right to speak up and speak out. To practice with this training on loving speech, I have had to pause and review when to speak and how to choose words that were truthful and kind. When all these conditions come together, my speech can be beneficial. After looking at whether these conditions are present, sometimes I speak and sometimes I don't. When I pause and inquire, I become aware of not just the words spoken, but also my intention and the consequence I hope to achieve with the words. Instead of this Training being a set of restrictions, it has given me a moment of insight to look at all the conditions when I am about to speak. It doesn't feel like I am suppressing my speech or being controlled by this guideline. Instead, it feels like a friend is reminding me of how I truly want to show up: with love and compassion. The pause and inquiry, each time I attempt to speak, has shifted my speech. This precept helps me to speak in a way that results in less regret. I don't have to spend time "mopping up" a mess caused by a moment when I was consumed by one emotion. Loving speech assures that we are practicing with the Noble Eightfold Path's step of Right Speech as our path of preventing further suffering in ourselves and others.

This Training connects closely to the second Training, True Happiness. When I am consumed by one emotion as a result of something that caused me pain or ill-being, it requires mindfulness to attend to the thought, word, or action that may be a reaction to the perceived source of that pain. When conditions are easeful and the mind is clear, I am more aware of my thoughts and the speech that might come from those thoughts. However, in a moment of hurt when I might be tired because it's been a long day, my mindfulness is also less present and I might react to my pain with anger, sadness, impatience, frustration, or hatred. Being mindful really matters so as not to generate more suffering through additional thoughts, speech, or writing that can increase the first moment of pain.

The Buddha's teaching on the first and second arrows can help us to understand this. The first arrow is the initial hurt. The second arrow is the emotional response to the hurt, which leads to more suffering. We get to be in choice when we maintain our mindfulness; we do not generate more suffering by mindfully taking care of the first arrow. In that moment of tiredness, I might entangle words said in the present moment with words from a past hurt, and this confusion can initiate pain, the second arrow. Right Effort and Right Mindfulness help me notice and make efforts to maintain a beneficial emotion that comes up, such as patience, or transform a difficult emotion such as impatience.

The Fifth Mindfulness Training

Nourishment and Healing

Aware of the suffering caused by unmindful consumption, I am committed to cultivating good health, both physical and mental, for myself, my family, and my society by practicing mindful eating, drinking, and consuming. I will practice looking deeply into how I consume the Four Kinds of Nutriments, namely edible foods, sense impressions, volition, and consciousness. I am determined not to gamble, or to use alcohol, drugs, or any other products which contain toxins, such as certain websites, electronic games, TV programs, films, magazines, books, and conversations. I will practice coming back to the present moment to be in touch with the refreshing, healing, and nourishing elements in me and around me, not letting regrets and sorrow drag me back into the past nor letting anxieties, fear, or craving pull me out of the present moment. I am determined not to try to cover up loneliness, anxiety, or other suffering by losing myself in consumption. I will contemplate interbeing and consume in a way that preserves peace, joy, and well-being in my body and consciousness, and in the collective body and consciousness of my family, my society, and the earth.

Valerie:

This Training, or precept, focuses on avoiding the consumption of intoxicants and other substances that cause harm to the body and the mind. From a broad perspective based in the Plum Village tradition, this precept is about how and what we consume.

Years ago, when I moved out of Brooklyn to Bucks County, Pennsylvania, I was disoriented in every sense of the word. In the city, there was a predictable pattern of life: the sounds of the elevated train and my neighbor's hip-hop music seeped through the paper-thin walls of my apartment, as did the gritty smells of the city itself. Now, as a new homeowner with a small lawn, I decided to orient myself in this new world of Bucks County by planting a flower garden, but I had no clue where or how to begin.

At first, I talked with people in the grocery stores and stopped to ask people in my neighborhood whose gardens I admired. Then I sought out training, which began with a year-long biodynamic gardening and farming program at the Pfeiffer Center (now Threefold Community Farm) in Chestnut Ridge, New York, and the Master Gardening Program at Rutgers University, New Jersey. What began as a curiosity to learn how to plant a garden has become an intense passion to understand myself and the natural world. Over time, my mindset shifted from what I could do with my small lawn to a sense of interrelationship with the earth; a kinship rooted in respect and reciprocity; an ethical and moral relationship of generosity, gratitude, and love. I began to understand that I had absorbed a whole belief system, largely unconsciously, from my upbringing in Brooklyn: to fear nature, to see myself as separate from the natural world. I had absorbed a consumptive and extractive mindset, viewing the natural world in terms of what I could consume or extract, largely blind to the short- and long-term costs.

I am aware that social inequities experienced by marginalized people are not separate from the fragmentation and disconnection from the natural world that is so rampant in society. I am aware that systems of domination like colonization, capitalism, and patriarchy contribute to domination and objectification, which feeds a hyper-consumptive and extractive mindset. What is needed, at least in part, to heal this disconnection is reciprocity, accountability, and reconciliation, as well as an emotional, ethical, and embodied connection to the earth. This was my mindset when, this spring, I was out picking ramps, a rare wild allium ephemeral that grows in wooded areas. The following day, I returned to the same wooden path and admired the forest floor full of spring ramps. A part of me wanted to harvest more. I felt the energy of grasping, wanting, with full awareness that the season for these coveted wild delicacies is so very brief.

Then, I recalled Robin Wall Kimmerer's concept of the "Honorable Harvest," indigenous ethical guidelines for taking from the earth that emphasize a reciprocal relationship of respect, gratitude, and sustainability; to take only what is needed and leave the rest.[16] I realized that my urge to take more was driven by a scarcity mindset, fear, and the desire to control. I paused, noticed the urge, and felt the tension in my body. I recognized that the ramps are sentient beings with intrinsic value. They are not an object to satisfy my urge for consumption. They exist in a complex and interdependent world that includes me. At that moment, I didn't see myself as separate from the ramps but instead as an expression of them. Their ability to thrive on the forest floor supports my ability to thrive. They are a manifestation of the abundance of spring; they are a gift. Acknowledging ramps as a gift shifted my mindset from extractive and consumptive to one of kinship, reciprocity, enoughness, and satisfaction. I walked back home with a sense of mutual flourishing: the ramps remained rooted on the forest floor, where they could thrive, and I felt rooted in gratitude, savoring the freedom to choose from the heart.

We consume all day long through the sense organs of eyes, ears, nose, mouth, body, and mind. In some cases, we have little control over what we consume, as in the case of seeing large billboards on public streets. In other cases, we have significant control over what we consume, such as if we have the socio-economic means to select a healthy, plant-based diet. Depending on where we live, access to consume healthy foods and therefore make healthy choices may be limited or nearly unlimited. Even among people who are materially well-off, many live in hypervigilance and fear because of social group identity: immigrants, BIPOC, LGBTQIA+, people with disabilities, and others with historically socially marginalized identities, which frequently causes people to fall into a scarcity mindset. Such hypervigilance is exacerbated by a global mental health crisis characterized by an increased sense of social isolation, polarization, anxiety, overwhelm, and depression, feeding a loneliness epidemic and us-against-them thinking. We might adopt the false notion that our access and therefore our choices are restrained. Yet, as I will share at the end of this chapter from Victor Frankl and Howard Thurman—two men who lived in brutal social conditions—one of our cherished freedoms is our power to listen for what is genuine in ourselves, as well as to choose how we think about a situation—our mindset—and to choose our own way, guided by ethical and moral values.

Marisela:

The Fifth Mindfulness Training, Nourishment and Healing, is another wonderful way to practice with choice and perceived lack of choice. When I first received transmission of this Training in 2002, I returned home and immediately stopped drinking alcohol. Until then, I was a moderate alcohol drinker. I drank every evening for "stress relief" and often drank more on the weekends to "unwind." During my adolescence I consumed lots of alcohol, mostly on weekends, and this lasted well into my thirties. So, it was big for me to return home from a five-day retreat, after receiving transmission of the Training, and immediately stop a lifelong practice of alcohol consumption. And yet it was easy.

This guideline was the friend inviting me into choice. It became clear to me that I had choice in determining whether I would continue to use alcohol in the way I had been using it my entire life. I could see that when I drank alcohol, I was less able to perceive clearly whether I was practicing deep listening and loving speech. I saw that alcohol was the grease that slid me into sexual relationships without first building a foundation of trust. Alcohol also dulled my ability to see clearly whether I was practicing respect and reverence for my life and the lives of others with the words I used, the way I behaved, and especially in my thinking. Drinking alcohol gave me a pass to ignore all the Trainings. I quickly decided that my commitment to following these Trainings required a clear head and mind. Therefore all forms of intoxicants had to go. Since that realization and my energetic attempt at acting into the Trainings, my life is more simple. There is a relaxation that comes from a platform of virtue, which the Trainings provide. When there is rest, there is more clarity, which leads to less chaos, fewer distractions, and greater spaciousness in both my mind and body. This dwelling place allows me to see what is needed for healing and attend appropriately toward the divine.

Each day is a new day to greet these Five Mindfulness Trainings and thank them for being in my life. With the Trainings, I feel ready to face myself and the world, equipped to remember this path that I want to be on and how I can do it each moment, each day. These Trainings help me live into the Five Spiritual Powers, Six Paramitas, and Four Noble Truths. They help me attempt to abide in the divine abodes—the Immeasurable Minds of kindness, compassion, sympathetic joy, and equanimity. It is a comfort to know that there is the light of the Trainings enlarging the light I already have inside. I remain with gratitude as I continue to heal, gain small moments of insight, and share out the benefit of this light to the world.

The Five Mindfulness Trainings Deepen All Other Wisdom Teachings

Marisela:

It is a gift to have guidelines or precepts that help us train our mind toward perfect understanding and love in this lifetime. They are like good friends who remind us what it is that we value and how we want to be in any moment, and they are consistently by our side. These friends help us remember to think, speak, and act in ways that prevent us from cultivating the dis-ease that sometimes leads to regret and harm in ourselves and others. The Buddha taught that spiritual friendships support our growth in virtue and keep us on the spiritual path. The Five Mindfulness Trainings have been a spiritual friend on this path of healing for me. They are like the friend you turn to when you want to check in on something you are thinking of doing, about to say, etc. When I have a question as to how to respond to something hurtful for example, I might check in with a friend, share with them the context, and listen to their counsel. The Five Mindfulness Trainings can be like this for you, too. You do a mental check in with them as you remember that you want to use compassionate speech—the Fourth Training—even when someone is rude in their speech to you. A friend we seek counsel from is someone we trust, someone who *lives* a wisdom tradition in such a way that we see their wisdom showing up in their way of being and doing. The Trainings also reflect and are, either directly or indirectly, part of other deep Buddhist teachings guiding us toward clarity and understanding.

The Teaching on the Four Establishments of Mindfulness

For example, the Five Mindfulness Trainings help us ground the teachings from the Buddha's Discourse on the Four Establishments of Mindfulness in our daily life—our mindfulness of our body, our feelings, our mind, and our objects of mind, such as thoughts and emotions—to develop a wholesome and happy state of mind.[17] Mindfulness is the ability to be present for what is with us and allows us to remember to practice with our precepts. The Four Establishments of Mindfulness help us become aware, with clear understanding, of what is happening in our body, feelings, mental formations, and consciousness. When we move about, we notice if our body is filled with tension or is at ease; we notice whether the actions of our body are kind or not. When we speak, we notice if our words are kind or not, and if the thoughts that produced our words were kind. We notice the perceptions formed when we come into contact with someone, and we ask ourselves if those perceptions are based on a past experience or if we are fully present to what is here right now. And we notice the mind that is conjuring up data for us to form these perceptions. In this way, we are able to discern how we are showing up for ourselves and others. This important teaching is the foundation for our path to awakening and helps us stay in awareness of the precepts in our daily life. The Five Mindfulness Trainings are our everyday life, not something we practice only when we meet in a sangha or go on a retreat. In this way, the Trainings are a direct action of the Four Establishments of Mindfulness and vice versa; they rest on one another.

The Teaching on the Six Paramitas

The Six Paramitas, or Perfections, are known in Buddhism as a path leading us to becoming a bodhisattva. A bodhisattva is a being who is on the path of perfecting the way of helping all beings become awakened, after perfecting the way in themself. In Mahayana Buddhism, the Six Paramitas are typically understood as generosity, ethical conduct/mindfulness, patience/inclusiveness, diligence, meditation, and wisdom. In the Plum Village Community of Engaged Buddhism, the Five Mindfulness Trainings are considered to be similar to the Paramita of ethical conduct as defined by many different Buddhist traditions.

Through our daily actions of body, speech, and thinking, we can bring much beauty and kindness into the world. Yet, on a daily basis, we often find ourselves regretting something we did, said, or thought. Sometimes we say or do things that cause harm, and we may recognize the harm immediately or may not become aware of the harm until a later time. Thích Nhất Hạnh taught that precepts are meant not to restrict us but to help us wake up from our ignorance. The precepts can be understood as an observer that assures we are waking up in each moment, again and again. The Trainings invite us into an awareness that is preventive; it prevents us from causing harm. Our ethical behavior ensures protection. When we act in line with the Trainings, we know we are on a path that is the antidote to harming in our thinking, speaking, and acting. With this awareness we can choose to act, speak, and think into existence a world that is based on our ethical principles. We can make these choices in large and small ways, in each moment of our lives. Our engagement with the Mindfulness Trainings helps us to continuously perfect our path toward greater understanding and love, and to live into our bodhisattva ideals moment by moment.

The Teaching on the Five Spiritual Powers

The Buddhist teaching of the Five Spiritual Powers also incorporates the Five Mindfulness Trainings. The Five Spiritual Powers are faith, diligence/energy, mindfulness, concentration, and insight. Here, again, mindfulness plays an important role. Mindfulness is at the center, balancing faith with insight and diligence, or energy with right concentration. We have faith in our path of liberation because each time we see the benefit of our practice, we gain more confidence that we are on the right path. We experience our faith in action, which reaffirms our faith. This experiential knowledge then gives us energy to practice with more diligence. We want to persist because we know that when we act and speak and think with awareness of our precepts, something beneficial occurs. The path empowers us as we see its effects in our daily life.

Our practice of the Mindfulness Trainings also keeps us balanced and leads us to slow down, to pause. In this pause, we see even more deeply the benefit of the Trainings; we see what leads to certain ways of thinking and where we can change our thoughts. We pause and notice what fuels our ignorance and our perception of separation, inferiority, and superiority. We become focused and concentrated during our pause as we find ease in our body and mind. When we pause, our thoughts and our body's energy settle down, like particles settling in a glass of cloudy water when it sits on a countertop for a few minutes. When things settle, we see what was always there, which was obscured by the particles in the glass or the distracted thoughts and energies in our body. Our concentration allows us to listen more deeply to what is inside of us. We listen to what is there, inside and outside of us, from a place of calm and ease, when things are more settled in mind and body. From this clear seeing, we gain insight into things that may have been clouded over. We may have insight into the root of a habitual behavior that consistently causes us harm that we may not have understood previously. Or we might gain insights that help us better understand our close ones.

With this clear understanding, we can learn how to engage with them more skillfully to avoid causing suffering. We help ourselves and each other find happiness where previously it seemed nonexistent or not possible. This is the power of faith, energy, mindfulness, concentration, and insight. As we enact these Five Spiritual Powers through the Trainings, we can continuously develop them and remain steady on our path of love and understanding.

Thầy reminds us that the precepts contain wisdom, which is like a light illuminating any confusion in our minds and guiding us on the path toward love and understanding.[18] We are lucky to always have such light showing us a way through the darkness of our mind when it is clouded by ignorance. Therefore, we must remember that even in moments of despair, when we wonder what our purpose is in this life form, and when we feel alone and confused, there is a light that shines brightly. This is our light of freedom that reminds us we are never alone, we are purposed and in choice, and we are here for a reason. The light of the Trainings is igniting our internal light to brighten the path of illumination for ourselves and for all beings.

The Teachings on the Four Noble Truths and the Noble Eightfold Path

After the Buddha experienced enlightenment under the bodhi tree, he set out to teach this path of enlightenment to others. The first Dharma talk he shared with the five ascetics, his companions prior to his enlightenment, presented the widely experienced Four Noble Truths. They are: acknowledging that ill-being exists, abandoning the path leading to ill-being, realizing the end of ill-being, and developing the path leading to the end of ill-being. This path leading to the end of ill-being is called the Noble Eightfold Path. The path begins with Right View because we must understand that the path will lead us to develop wisdom. With this right view of the teaching of the Four Noble Truths, our thinking then guides our speech, action, and livelihood. As with many Buddhist teachings, mindfulness is an important element of the eightfold path that leads to the end of suffering. Along with Right View and Right Mindfulness, the other elements are Right Thought, Right Speech, Right Action, Right Livelihood, Right Effort, and Right Concentration; these lead us to insight, or wisdom, which ends our perception of ill-being.

The practice of this path requires Right Mindfulness, which is nourished by Right Effort, the effort to be aware of the five hindrances that block us from following the path. These hindrances are described as sensual desire, aversion, sloth and torpor (also called dullness and drowsiness), restlessness and worry, and delusion. With Right Effort, we are able to prevent the hindrances from arising or remove them when they arrive, and we can nourish or bring forward the antidotes to the hindrances. These antidotes include: awareness that all things are impermanent and changing; development of practices that bring forth loving kindness; and finding a balance between the extremes of sloth and torpor on the one hand, and restlessness and worry on the other hand, so we have sufficient energy to practice while investigating the roots of our doubt. With Right Effort, Right Mindfulness persists and leads to a concentrated mind that is able to see clearly and develop insight into all phenomena. Thầy often emphasized that mindfulness, concentration, and insight (*smṛti*, *samadhi*, and *prajna* in Sanskrit) are the basic practices for much of our Plum Village tradition; they inter-are, and they lead us on the path of awakening.

The Five Mindfulness Trainings put into action the Noble Eightfold Path through daily right actions of non-killing, non-stealing, sexual responsibility, right speech, and right consumption of all nutriments.

The Five Mindfulness Trainings Cultivate Our Internal Guidance

Valerie:

The word *precept* comes from the Latin *praeceptum*, meaning rule or command. It is derived from the verb *praecipere*, which combines *prae* (before) and *capere* (to take). This suggests instruction in advance, sometimes called warm instruction. Essentially, precepts are principles or rules that guide action or behavior of a moral, ethical, or instructional nature. From a Buddhist perspective, the precepts, or Five Mindfulness Trainings, are the foundation for living an awakened, wholesome, compassionate, and peaceful life. The power of these precepts stems from their internalization *before* we take action. In other words, we live our daily life and make choices—from the friends we keep, to the food we eat, to the content we absorb—all guided by our understanding of the precepts.

In the Plum Village community, we are encouraged to read the trainings out loud regularly every month or more frequently, with our sangha or by ourselves, reflecting on how we have or have not applied the teachings in the past few weeks. This iterative process of deep looking is where we come to really digest the mindfulness trainings' relevance to our life in concrete terms—not in the abstract. It is important to keep reminding ourselves of the language of the precepts as we put them into practice.

Perhaps the first step in practicing the precepts in daily life begins with the practice of *samatha*, or stopping. Rather than moving on autopilot, we pause and reflect on the choices in front of us and make a choice that aligns with our values, guided by the precepts. We have the capacity to make deliberate decisions, led by the Trainings, once we have internalized them through study, reflection, and examination—*before* we take action.

We practice with the precepts on three levels: the level of awareness or attention; the level of stabilizing the mind and body through mindfulness, concentration, and insight; and the level of intention or volition. At the first level, in meditation practice, we bring our awareness and attention to this moment. This could mean we are watching the in- and out-breath or being aware of taking a step, tasting a carrot, or looking up at the sky. We are aware of this moment, knowing that it is impermanent, in flux. Awareness becomes stabilized with concentration, which in turn supports being present for this moment. Stabilizing our mind and nervous system supports inner groundedness. Our beliefs, actions, and body responses are shaped by the stability of our nervous system. A nervous system in dysregulation is going to create dysregulated thoughts, actions, and relationships. The quality of groundedness and stability through concentration makes it possible to tolerate challenging emotions and thoughts. With this anchor of concentration of body and mind, a quality of insight can arise. We are in a position to know how we feel, understand the nature of our environment, and know how to act.

With these qualities of awareness and stability of mind, we can reflect on our intention, or volition, which Thầy says is the very ground of all our actions. Living an intentional life guided by the precepts is the essence of the Buddhist teachings. Intention is considered an important nutriment, as important as food and water. We consume our volition daily, along with the three other types of nutriments that were explained by the Buddha: edible foods; sense impressions we receive through the sense organs of our eyes, ears, skin, and mind; and consciousness. For many, intention can feel slippery; first it's this, then it's that. Others are quite certain of their intention. Yet intention is not a precision tool. It is the effort to name our intention that is instructive and important. Our Buddhist practice teaches us to examine our volition, or intention, let it spring from a heart of love, and be faithful to the call from within. Living with volition invites us to take an inventory of our thoughts and actions and to test whether they are in alignment with our values, with the precepts, and with other Buddhist teachings such as the Noble Eightfold Path.

Here is an example of how I approach these three levels of practicing in my own life. One of my deepest intentions is to prioritize social connections and relationships. This is a reversal of how I spent many years in my legal career, placing work above my personal life and social connections. I begin by noticing the quality of my awareness: Am I being pulled in too many directions? Do I feel stressed? On a very basic level, I pause and simply check in with myself. This moment of pause creates stability and space that supports a quality of grounded awareness. From this regulated place, I call to mind the Trainings, my values, and my intention to prioritize social connections. How do I live this aspiration? How do I communicate about it? What action is needed now? How do I choose?

The precepts rest within other Buddhist teachings that include the Four Noble Truths, the Noble Eightfold Path, the Six Paramitas, the Five Spiritual Powers, and the Four Immeasurable Minds. Each of these teachings form the basis for cultivating a mindset inclined toward compassion, peace, love and understanding. They form a firm foundation for developing a state of mind that is nourishing for us and for society. For example, when we understand that the nature of living this human life is that we are vulnerable, and that we and everyone we love will eventually become sick and die, we begin to understand a very real truth about suffering. There is suffering; the nature of being is the nature of dying. No one can escape that reality.

Allegiances to the precepts are formed in many ways: for example, through our family of origin, our communities, our faith groups, our peers, our workplaces, and society at large. With reflection and inquiry, we can gain awareness of whether or not our mind states and behaviors align with these precepts. By their nature, precepts help deter harmful conduct and follow the bodhisattva path. Two examples in my own life come to mind. First, I value good health, a plant-based diet, and a fair and livable wage for the people who grow the food I eat and so forth. I do my best to avoid eating ultra-processed foods on a regular basis. It might be fast and convenient but in the long term, compromises my health and well-being. Second, I place a high value on engaging in Right Livelihood, which means work that is in service to others, promotes peace and justice in the world, and creates greater compassion and understanding. Often, I am called to test my alignment to that value in choosing the work that I say yes to. Before I take on a project, I reflect on how it aligns with my values: promoting peace and social justice, for example. When I was working as a lobbyist-lawyer, I held very different values. My values were to make money, earn praise, get promoted, and get ahead in my career. I was unaware of the precepts or any Buddhist teachings, and my values were largely driven by external forces. I was driven by what Buddhism calls the eight worldly winds: gain, loss, fame, disgrace, blame, praise, pleasure, and pain. These "winds" rest on an overreliance on the outer world and the beliefs that we are separate from each other and that things are permanent and unchanging. I want to acknowledge that to be able to do this type of reflection is a great privilege. I am aware that many people have, or believe they have, limited choices. They may have young children or elderly parents to support or other responsibilities that restrict the choices they can make, or believe they can make. Yet, even with these limitations or constraints, all of us can be conscious of the choices we make.

The invitation is to cultivate over time a state of mind inclined toward the precepts as both a teacher, guide, and source of confidence in sense making and choice making. When life is confusing and chaotic and we don't know what to do (and that happens frequently in my life), pausing to reflect deeply on precepts can provide guidance. When we apply them to our daily life on a consistent basis, they enable our actions to be guided by wisdom: the ability to make healthy and life-affirming choices based on our bodhisattva ideal and understanding. Precepts help us restore balance in our lives and offer caution when we are at a crossroads.

Precepts, or Trainings, are not only about ethics individually and collectively; they are also the basis for a compassionate and just society. When we adopt a precept-inclined state of mind, we practice noticing our states of mind. Our consciousness produces actions. For example, I notice when I have a mind state that is embedded with kindness, I hold doors open for others and offer a smile to strangers on the street. The practice is to notice our current mind states and cultivate states of mind that are beneficial for us individually and for society collectively.

We sometimes underestimate the importance of the ability to choose a particular state of mind. Throughout history, many figures have offered guidance about the power of our capacity and freedom to choose. For example, Victor Frankl was an Austrian neurologist, psychologist, philosopher, and

Holocaust survivor who founded logotherapy, a school of psychotherapy that describes a search for life's meaning as humans' central motivational force. Frankl famously said:

> everything can be taken from a man but one thing: the last of the human freedoms—to choose one's attitude in any given set of circumstances, to choose one's own way.[19]

Similarly, Howard Thurman—an American author, philosopher, theologian, Christian mystic, educator, and civil rights leader—was guided by a set of precepts embedded in his spiritual life. He believed that his connection to God could happen anywhere and in everything he did. In one of his most famous speeches, given at Spelman College in 1980, Thurman said:

> There is something in every one of you that waits, listens, for the sound of the genuine in yourself. And if you cannot hear it, you will never find whatever it is for which you're searching. And if you hear it and then do not follow it, it were better that you had never been born....
>
> You are the only you that has ever lived. Your idiom is the only idiom of its kind in all the existences. And if you cannot hear the sound of the genuine in you, you will all of your life spend your days on the ends of strings that somebody else pulls.[20]

To develop a precept-inclined mind state is to cultivate self-examination and self-reflection in order to recall the precepts we have inherited from our family of origin, our society, our inner values, and Buddhist teachings. And we cannot do this examination alone. We need the support and guidance of a community or practitioners. The precepts, or Trainings, are realized not in the abstract but through practice, not only as individuals, but in community.

3

Living the Contemplations on the Five Mindfulness Trainings

Valerie:

Thích Nhất Hạnh framed the Five Mindfulness Trainings in positive language: "Aware of the suffering caused by..." as opposed to "I vow not to..." Thầy's recasting of the original precepts in these Trainings points the way not only to an ethical and moral pathway but also to the power to take responsibility for our thoughts and actions. In this way we enter a more wholesome, living relationship with ourselves, others, and the world.

In the United States, the political landscape has changed dramatically since 2020, and that brief period of racial reckoning that followed the murder of George Floyd. Today, in the US, we have seen the dismantling of DEI initiatives throughout public and private sectors, coming under attack as "woke" and therefore suspect. The public landscape is in crisis. Many people point to a kind of moral injury that is reflected in increased rates of depression and anxiety, feelings of loneliness and isolation, and decreased trust in one another. Today, with the polarization, isolation, and divisiveness happening in the United States and worldwide, I sense that the Contemplations are needed now more than ever as a bridge of healing and understanding.

We continue to rely on the Five Mindfulness Trainings as the foundation for living an ethical life. Under these current conditions, the Contemplations and accompanying mindfulness practices provide a new interpretation and ethical road map, especially for community organizers, social activists, and historically socially marginalized people who are often on the front lines of social change. For example, I was recently invited to offer a mindfulness program to a group of Black lawyers working at an international law firm. These Black lawyers are advocates for DEI and environmental justice in their professional lives. The current federal administration has specifically targeted such lawyers, working on issues of environmental justice and DEI in Big Law firms. Needless to say, these lawyers were stressed from the frontal assault on the very work that they were trained to do—to protect civil rights, civil liberties, and the DEI programs which are designed to promote fair treatment and equal opportunity for all individuals. They were burned out by a near-constant vigilance that threatened their very legitimacy as lawyers, the politics of navigating workspaces, and the real effort and skill required to engage in hard conversations amidst the divisiveness. They asked me to offer a meditation practice that might help them calm their nervous systems and offer them a glimpse of peace. At the end of our time together, which was a very abbreviated thirty-minute session, they said the peaceful pause really helped and brought them "back home" to a sense of themselves.

This is the power of mindfulness, concentration, and insight, which can be felt and experienced right away. We offer these Contemplations on the Five Mindfulness Trainings as a manifesto for present action and a tribute. They are a manifesto of the spirit of love in action and compassion, and at the same time, they represent our love and respect for the Five Mindfulness Trainings as a foundation for an ethical and loving global society. As we live out the Five Mindfulness Trainings in our daily life, they become a living record of our practice.

As mentioned previously in this book, the Contemplations are *not* meant to displace or replace the Five or Fourteen Mindfulness Trainings. We are deeply grateful to Thầy and the Plum Village community for the Five and the Fourteen Mindfulness Trainings, upon which the Contemplations rest. For those new to practicing with written contemplations, they are meant to be engaged together with the Five and/or Fourteen Mindfulness Trainings. We think many people will get the most from this book by reading, studying, reflecting, realizing, applying, practicing, and transforming with both the Contemplations and the Five and Fourteen Mindfulness Trainings. We saw a need to address and speak directly to people who are often systemically marginalized, based on our own lived experience. For those familiar with the Five and Fourteen Mindfulness Trainings, we encourage you to continue to read, study, reflect, realize, apply, practice, and transform with them, and to engage the Contemplations as a way of deepening your understanding of the Trainings.

—

The current version of the Contemplations on the Five Mindfulness Trainings, presented below, is an updated version of the ones published in 2020. We hope this shortened form will allow for greater accessibility.

Contemplations on the Five Mindfulness Trainings

Preamble to the Contemplations on the Five Mindfulness Trainings

Let us open to another way of understanding the Five Mindfulness Trainings, guiding principles for mindful and ethical living, which call us toward individual and collective awakening, compassion, and peace. We are interconnected. What happens in one part of the universe affects people everywhere. What happens to the Black body affects all bodies. We are called forward.

Global pandemics, the climate crisis, and social and economic oppression and upheaval are gateways to suffering worldwide, disproportionately impacting Black, Indigenous, and other people of color; people with disabilities; people currently and historically subject to poverty, war, and genocide; LGBTQIA+ people; people facing health inequities and premature death; people facing generational displacement; and people with historically socially marginalized identities, including those facing oppression because of their abilities, gender, or immigration status. They, we, are not alone. Our lives and livelihoods are interconnected. We are called forward.

We cannot exist independent of, for example, low-wage workers, health care workers, unhoused people, single mothers, undocumented people, the unemployed and underemployed, and similarly situated people. If one such person lives on the knife edge of racial, ethnic, social, structural, and systemic oppression and discrimination, we are all affected. We are called forward.

The practitioner dwells in the now, recognizing the dualistic nature of equanimity and instability, discrimination and nondiscrimination, ill-being and well-being. We practice Right View and compassionate action, moving toward Right Insight. Aware of the interconnectedness and interdependence of all life, we courageously turn to practice wholeheartedly. We are called forward.

Lighting a stick of incense, listening to the sutras, sitting upright and solid, palms joined, the practitioner looks within, and in concentration the path and fruit of skillful action are revealed. We are called forward.

Speak aloud these words with the sangha voice, a true river of understanding.

Contemplation on the First Mindfulness Training: Acknowledging Beauty as Reverence for Life

Aware of the suffering caused by oppression and generational harm based on racial, cultural, social, and ethnic inferiority and superiority, I acknowledge the beauty and violence inherent in life. I vow to resist being complicit in systems and structures that continue to perpetuate injustice, violence, hatred, and delusion instead of reverence of life for marginalized groups and others. I recognize that each person contributes to my individual and our collective awakening, and to the co-creation of a world that celebrates and affirms differences and similarities. All living beings can teach me something, when I remember to pause, breathe, listen deeply with a calm and open mind and heart, and ask myself, "Is there more?" or "What else is here with me?" I honor and respect all life, guided by Right View and Right Effort.

Contemplation on the Second Mindfulness Training: Belonging and Connecting as True Happiness

Aware of the suffering caused by ignorance and aversion of my own and others' racial, ethnic, cultural, and social history, its legacy and how this affects me, I am committed to learning and connecting to these histories. Aware that there is no genetic or biological difference among racial and ethnic groups, and that these identities were socially constructed by one group to establish dominance over others, I will turn toward all forms of othering with the aspiration of transforming heart and mind. I know that this history has led to fragmentation inside and outside the body and mind and has brought much suffering to all beings. I will notice when emotions of belonging and othering arise, and I will ask myself, "Why?" Whatever feelings, perceptions, or mental formations arise in me, I will embrace and engage them with love in action. I am committed to practicing Right Resolve, Right Speech, Right Action, and Right Livelihood so I can help relieve this legacy of racial and social suffering. I will practice looking deeply to see that true happiness is not possible without true connection leading to belonging and understanding.

Contemplation on the Third Mindfulness Training: Cherishment as True Love

Aware of the suffering caused by discrimination and oppression, I vow to transform these seeds in myself, my sangha, and society. I recognize the ways in which I have benefitted or not benefitted, explicitly or implicitly, from systems and structures of injustice. I am aware of the legacy of violence, including unlawful police violence, perpetrated against people of various gender identities, expressions, and sexual orientations, Black people, indigenous people, people of color, people with disabilities, undocumented people, people suffering mental health challenges, and others who are marginalized. I am committed to looking tenderly at my suffering, knowing that I am not separate from others and that the seeds of suffering contain the seeds of joy. I am aware that narrow interpretations of intimate relationships constrain how we cherish each other in our expression of love, leaving many isolated and alienated. I celebrate bold love that fosters compassion, justice, and peace, and tender love that seeks understanding. I cherish this breath, body, mind, and moment as an act of healing for myself and for others. I cherish the liberation of all beings guided by the wisdom and the solidity of the sangha as my path of true love.

Contemplation on the Fourth Mindfulness Training: Vulnerability as Deep Listening and Loving Speech

Aware that vulnerability is the essence of our true nature, our humanness, I vow to risk listening for understanding rather than disagreement. I am committed to generous and courageous listening that bridges differences and supports others who may be different from me. When I am not able to understand others, I vow to come back to my breath and my body, and to offer myself gentle patience. I am aware that loving communication rests on honesty, compassion, and openness that align with my highest aspiration to alleviate suffering. When I have hurt others through my unskillful listening or speech, I vow to practice true beneficial regret, making a good apology that acknowledges what I have done and the harm caused, accepting responsibility and being accountable for my behavior, and offering sincere regret for my actions, knowing that this supports the other person and me. Through my practices of vulnerability, forgiveness, and deep listening, I know that my speech will be guided by love and understanding. Practicing in this way supports Right Speech and Right Action and guides me to Right Insight.

Contemplation on the Fifth Mindfulness Training: Welcoming as True Nourishing and Healing

Aware of the suffering caused by the consumption of an inadequate history of racial and ethnic forms of social segregation and injustice, I am committed to healing myself and the world. I am aware that my thoughts, perceptions, feelings, words, and actions may have been influenced by this history. I vow to understand how I have been influenced by embracing and denying this racial, social, and ethnic history of inferiority, superiority, and equality. I will cultivate joy to nourish me in this aspiration. I will practice mindfulness of the Four Kinds of Nutriments to become aware of how edible foods, sense impressions, volition, and consciousness are all influenced by this history. Practicing with Right Energy and Right Resolve, my conscious consumption will be guided by Right Action that welcomes differences without discrimination. This Right Insight offers true welcoming on this path to nourish and heal myself, my ancestors, my descendants, my sangha, and society.

The Five Mindfulness Trainings keep us centered in life's storms and joys and remind us that life is a precious gift. The Trainings are a path to liberation and transformation. Practicing these Trainings supports us toward racial and ethnic reconciliation and social change and heals deep suffering. The Five Mindfulness

Trainings help us cross this shore of suffering and bring us to the side of true awakening and love. The Contemplations on the Five Mindfulness Trainings are a commentary to these foundational teachings and are meant to offer another way of understanding Thích Nhất Hạnh's teachings to live an ethical life.

We are called forward.

Contemplation on the First MindfulnessTraining

Acknowledging Beauty as Reverence for Life

Aware of the suffering caused by oppression and generational harm based on racial, cultural, social, and ethnic inferiority and superiority, I acknowledge the beauty and violence inherent in life. I vow to resist being complicit in systems and structures that continue to perpetuate injustice, violence, hatred, and delusion instead of reverence of life for marginalized groups and others. I recognize that each person contributes to my individual and our collective awakening, and to the co-creation of a world that celebrates and affirms differences and similarities. All living beings can teach me something, when I remember to pause, breathe, listen deeply with a calm and open mind and heart, and ask myself, "Is there more?" or "What else is here with me?" I honor and respect all life, guided by Right View and Right Effort.

Marisela:

This first Contemplation is one that keeps resonating again and again. It restores me and reminds me that I am beautiful.

It helps me turn to and repair some of the harm done by the social norms stating that only some people are beautiful and worthy of reverence. Growing up, and into young adulthood, I always felt ugly. I have a gap between my top front teeth and was always reminded that this was ugly, definitely abnormal. My smile was not a full smile. Beauty as reverence for life reminds me that to revere myself and others like me, I must embrace my "beauty," inside and out. For many, the dualistic nature of beauty and ugliness is matched to good and bad, right and wrong. In times of despair, I have allowed seeds of "ugly, bad, and wrong" to take up a whole lot of space in me. It was and is easy to feel ugly and wrong and inferior in a world that relegates white, heterosexual, US-born, male-bodied, wealthy, and other such identities as superior, beautiful, good, and powerful. Looking beyond this dualism, I feel content with myself, settled in, and grateful I have teeth that allow me to chew and nourish myself. I have reverence for the form and identities I am in this lifetime, and for the diversity of ways all forms show up. I practice regularly with touching the earth and releasing to the earth, water, sun, and wind elements, these unwholesome messages that have taken up space in me. I ask the elements to refresh me and transform these violent messages.

My acceptance of the beauty inside and outside of me has provided support for those holding similar perceptions of beauty in regard to having "gapped" teeth. At a recent retreat for BIPOC woman-identified people at the Garrison Institute, several people shared with me how happy they were to see me fully smiling in front of the sangha. Someone said, "I never thought I would see someone with your teeth co-leading a retreat and smiling so brightly." Someone wrote a poem about smiling with gapped teeth. I deeply felt the connection with these individuals as we were acknowledging this Training together: that we felt beautiful, and this embracing of all of ourselves was an acknowledgment of reverence for our lives. We were not less than people without gapped teeth. How wonderful it is to acknowledge truth and grow it together.

This perception of beauty is not only for this one feature of my body. It is for all of the forms I embody that have historically been cast as ugly, inferior, not revered, not respected, or unworthy. This includes the color of my skin, the texture of my hair, the shape and size of my eyes, nose, and lips, the height of my body, the size of my hips and waist, and the size of my breasts. Perceptions of beauty are also attributed to the way I speak, the accent that reveals itself when I am tired, the way I walk, the words I use, the experiences I have, the way I dance, the way I stand and sit. A social and cultural standard of beauty is designated by a group of people with that particular perception of beauty. Once I let go of these designations, in all their forms and renditions, a contentment took over. Beauty became a happiness, a contentment with what is, with my body and the way I show up. Sister Chân Đức—a respected elder in our Plum Village tradition, whose name means "True Virtue"—teaches that beauty is how we show up when we practice with fine manners, the "fine manners" being the ways in which monastics behave to cultivate peace, respect, and concentration, fostering a sacred atmosphere around themselves at all times. I find this to be beautiful. When I practice in a way that reveres me as a person with Buddha nature on this path of true love, I am beautiful and revered. I am enough.

Valerie:

> *Flowers are the prayers of the vegetal world. The plants offer their beauty to the Supreme.*
>
> —**The Mother,** *Flowers and Their Messages*

All my life I've been a sucker for beauty, especially beauty in the form of flowers, plants, and the natural world. I would rather go without food than without flowers. It sounds dramatic—and that's real for me. I recall a time years ago when I was desperate to touch the natural world. I was living in a third-floor walk-up hall room in Queens, working at Burger King, and going to City University of New York in Manhattan at night. On my way to school one day, I passed a street vendor selling roses by the bundle in colors of peach, scarlet, and magenta. Time stopped as I stared at them. I heard them whisper two words to every part of my body: "Take me."

In those days I had a skin-tight budget and lived mostly on chicken livers at less than one dollar for a small container, which I could buy at a cut-rate grocery store down the street. I looked at the flowers. They looked at me. I calculated the cost in my head. Twenty bucks. *TWENTY BUCKS*. I looked at the vendor, a savvy, street-smart Latinx man with a baby face and hefty hands. He saw my dilemma; he had seen this before. The flowers would cost my entire food budget for the week. I knew (and he knew) the flowers were outside my budget, but that was alright because I wasn't buying roses. I was buying the luxurious, overabundant desire to touch and smell something beautiful, like spring wind in a turquoise sky, warm rain pooling in the moonlight, or a slow lifting fog, and that was priceless, so the roses were a bargain.

Roses remind me of the importance of beauty for beauty's sake. Beauty is complete and gives generously. It is a homecoming that excavates an inner sensitivity and sureness that is present, waiting, and expectant. Growing up in Brooklyn, I knew the natural world was there, generous and beautiful, of course, but at that time it seemed distant, rough, and inaccessible. The gentle sun came up and set over the parched terrain of Bushwick's row homes, concrete sidewalks, and chain-link fences. To see and feel grass, my brothers Charles and Elliot and I would run through Evergreens Cemetery on Bushwick Avenue, one of the great urban forests of New York City, paying little or no mind to the lives marked by tombstones. We were there to smell the green, green grass and feel it squishy under our sneakers and get close to muscular trees like a hundred-year-old sweet gum, black oaks, and white ash trees. We were chasing an emerging feeling, a fleeting sense of the timeless present, moments that glow in their luminosity and cannot be possessed but are lived with a slower presence of the immediate now.

For me, this time spent at Evergreens was more than dodging city streets. I was safe among the trees and flowers emerging in the spring, and the leaves falling in autumn. They wanted nothing from me and gave me beauty not as a luxury concept but as a birthright to be known, felt, and lived. My mother, a single parent working two jobs to support four kids, took in boarders in our sturdy brick house with oak doors and beveled glass. She filled every room, including the tiny hall room, little more than a closet, with older alcoholic Black men who had seen better times. Innocent and available, I was left in the house and subjected to sexual abuse by these tenants until they left or ran out of money to pay rent. The terror of the abuse in this strange place was adjacent to the beauty of Evergreens, the daffodils and cherry blossoms in spring, the autumn leaves in full glorious color. Even with the terror, or perhaps because of it, I held on to the beauty of Evergreens that could not be damaged, destroyed, or diminished, that was beyond the physical landscape and pointed instead to a horizon within me, tranquil and unstained.

That moment with the street vendor years ago led me to a lifelong love of not just roses but also flower gardening (as I described earlier in the book). When I moved from Brooklyn into my barn-like home outside Philadelphia, and after my husband left and we divorced, I set out to create something beautiful from the death of the marriage, to transform the "mud" of the marriage into a "lotus" garden. To paraphrase Wendy Johnson, one of the founders of the Garden Program at Green Gulch Zen Center in California, there are three good reasons to grow flowers: for beauty, for the coming apart of beauty, and to begin again.[21] This wisdom aligns with many Buddhist teachings and, for me, especially the teachings on impermanence (*anitya*). The beauty of growing flowers is a living lesson on impermanence.

The Buddha asked all practitioners to manifest, moment-to-moment, the insight of impermanence. As a *Dharmacharya*, a Dharma teacher in the Plum Village tradition, I feel especially drawn to learn the inescapable reality of impermanence not as a theory but as an ongoing realization and practice I can share with others. Ultimately, everything and everyone changes despite sometimes resisting change. Flowers decompose; a child becomes an adult; day becomes night. This calls for practice with the shifting nature of reality: to love, to care, to accept, to occupy space and time, to release, to let go.

This loving and letting go is the essence of gardening, and it was a lesson I relearned in my garden through an old flowering *Wisteria sinensis*. When I moved into my home, the wisteria grew over the cottage roof and threatened to rip off the shingles with its branching, leafless, wooden tentacles. Slowly, little by little, I cut back the vine and trained it over a substantial wooden pergola. In late spring, the plant bloomed a voluptuous cascade of blue to purple flowers, perfuming the air. Impermanence teaches that things ripen, flower in their time, and fade away in a continuous cycle of beauty, being, becoming, and nonbeing. It teaches gratitude and appreciation for the unrepeating wonder of each day, each moment.

What have I learned from this experience? Because of impermanence, I have learned that I can change my relationship to the abuse that happened to me. I acknowledge the beauty and violence inherent in life. I am aware that the people who abused me were abused themselves and were caught in a system and structure that perpetuated their despair and degradation. I'm aware of both the violence I experienced and the beauty of the Evergreens. Today, both the beauty and the violence are available to support me in transforming my life to be of service to others, to grow compassion not only for myself but also for victims and perpetrators of violence and abuse.

Contemplation on the Second Mindfulness Training

Belonging and Connecting as True Happiness

Aware of the suffering caused by ignorance and aversion of my own and others' racial, ethnic, cultural, and social history, its legacy and how this affects me, I am committed to learning and connecting to these histories. Aware that there is no genetic or biological difference among racial and ethnic groups, and that these identities were socially constructed by one group to establish dominance over others, I will turn toward all forms of othering with the aspiration of transforming heart and mind. I know that this history has led to fragmentation inside and outside the body and mind and has brought much suffering to all beings. I will notice when emotions of belonging and othering arise, and I will ask myself, "Why?" Whatever feelings, perceptions, or mental formations arise, I will embrace and engage with love in action. I am committed to practicing Right Resolve, Right Speech, Right Action, and Right Livelihood so I can help relieve this legacy of racial and social suffering. I will practice looking deeply to see that true happiness is not possible without true connection leading to belonging and understanding.

Marisela:

This second Contemplation helps me to continue to understand and experience that true happiness is true connections, and allows me to sense into belonging anywhere I feel connected: with places, people, Mother Earth. It helps me remember that the individualistic culture of the United States and beyond is not what I want to nurture in me. I see more clearly that injustices of all forms, small (daily microaggressions) and large (genocide), can only occur because people feel completely separate from each other, and separate from the elements inside and outside of us—land, the water, the wind, and the sun. This apparent separation gives rise to a perceived freedom to take something—time, space, land, kindness, love—from me, from other people, from all sentient life forms, and from the elements: all for a perceived colonial settler's comfort or to fulfill an ideology of the dualistic notion of superiority and inferiority.

When I take time away from listening to and caring for myself in order to fulfill the colonial mindset of "stealing," "taking," "extracting," and "oppressing," sometimes I am still unable to connect inside this very form I was born into in this lifetime. This is the first non-belonging, or taking: I cannot belong to myself. In a world where there is ultimately no separation, we naturally understand that we belong to each other. But in the mundane or conventional world, where everyday movement through life requires attention and care to how this body functions, listening and connecting to the body is necessary for belonging, for happiness, for respect. With the practice of awareness and the action of respecting myself, I turn inward and notice. I embody my breath and let it tell me what is happening inside, what is needed for connection. This allows me to move through the world from an embodied state instead of my body being separate from my mind, with the mind always on and uninformed by my body. The embodied state is a deep connection, feeling into the tensions, the spaciousness, the stuckness, and the flow of energy in this body. It is a settling and a belonging.

The second taking occurs in the separation I feel from other human beings and how I use this feeling to justify taking from others—time, resources, love, kindness—in a way that expects some kind of reciprocity. The majority of us have been reared to believe relationships need to be transactional and to value this. Because of the clear separation installed through socialized, gendered, and sexual identities, and the way the majority of people conform to the structural and systemic roles and values attributed to these identities, it is easy to simply consider myself separate from the "other." It is "normal" to see my brown skin as separate and different from that of paler-skinned people, and previously, it was easy to believe in the dualism brought about by the global ideology of whiteness, which encouraged me to feel inferior to them. That same dualistic pattern also existed for other identities: female-bodied and male-bodied, immigrant and non-immigrant, queer and heterosexual. For me, feeling into this separation can even justify a righteous hating, a taking or stripping someone of their humanity: "Clearly it's okay because they have stripped me of my humanity." I see now that I can retaliate against a person in this way only when I see them as separate from me, without spaciousness to understand how their humanity is showing up and why. Because I have "othered" them, I lose the spaciousness to see their humanity and connect with their pain. They also were socialized and also require unlearning, like I do. We can belong to each other in a healthy and generative way that ushers in connection and understanding instead of competition and extraction.

The third taking comes from our human assumption that other-than-human life forms are inferior and therefore ours for the taking as we attempt to make our lives better. We have devolved into an Anthropocenic period where humans' activity has had destructive impacts on the natural environment. The animal, plant, insect, winged, and water creatures, great and small, are impacted. Their habitats have been destroyed or changed, and they have been dispossessed. It has been nonstop gentrification for the creatures on the planet. I, too, have contributed to this extraction as a human growing up and living in this period. This Contemplation continues to reconnect me to more-than-human life forms with respect and understanding that we are all part of the net of sentient beings. My vegetarian diet encourages me to be in greater awareness of all life forms. On occasions when I consume cheese, I look deeply to better understand how the taking of milk from a cow, sheep, or goat has deprived that animal. I try to recognize that through their milk products, I am now their continuation, and therefore we are connected and belong to each other. When a child receives milk from their mother, there is a transmission of energy between them. It is the same with the receipt of cheese, transformed from the milk of an animal. We inter-are.

While living at monasteries in the Plum Village tradition, I learned that before we cut flowers, we can bow to them and ask permission to cut them. We can acknowledge their life as connected to our life and celebrate how a flower is enhancing our lives. The flowers' beauty is already enough, and it benefits me even further when I cut and offer them to the Buddha or to others. Likewise, in many native Indigenous cultures, it is my understanding that they are aware of a deep connection between an animal and human life: we are relatives. Thus, when an animal gives up their life to nurture human lives, there might be an offering before the animal life is taken and an acknowledgment of the circle of life and how we honor this gift of nutriment.

The fourth taking occurs with the land and the natural elements of water, wind, and sun. We humans, including myself, have taken and extracted from the land and water for our own selfish purposes. We have devastated the climate through our use of energy sources, and we continue to do so. I am especially aware of the taking of land and waterways of Indigenous people in the Americas and across the world. Mahogany is near extinction from logging in parts of Central America, South America, and the Caribbean. Islands and glaciers are in crisis as one is taken over by the other's melting. Considering the ways I have benefited through my consumption as a human, I take responsibility for my part in this devastation and extraction, this dispossession from people like me and different from me. I vow to acknowledge the racial capitalism and colonial actions that continue to devastate the elements with no regard. I will play my part in understanding how my consumption can provide a market for continued taking, disconnecting, and non-belonging.

Whenever I drop into my interconnectedness with all life forms, this imprinted path of taking drops away and sharing emerges. This has become more and more a lived experience for me. When I dip my body into a stream, a river, a lake, or an ocean, I feel the water element in me merge with the water element outside of me. There is truly no separation as contentment, joy, and belonging settle in my mind and body. It becomes restful, and from there clarity is birthed. This connection and clarity leads me to see all the things that are already present for my happiness. The elements are in me; there is no separation. I just have to remember this, and when I do, I realize I belong to something so much greater than this single life form and this human species.

Valerie:

I walked slowly, mindfully, and took my seat at the front of the altar in the main meditation hall at Deer Park Monastery. I looked out onto the faces of hundreds of BIPOC practitioners attending a milestone twentieth-anniversary retreat. In that moment, a flash of memories came rushing back from twenty years before, in March 2004, when the Colors of Compassion Retreat was the first BIPOC retreat offered by Zen Master Thích Nhất Hạnh and Plum Village.

I had arrived a day early for the retreat. I flew into San Diego, where smog hung low as though the city were covered in cheesecloth. I got off the airport shuttle in downtown San Diego and found a $45-a-night room that included breakfast in a seedy hotel, across from a strip mall and a fast-food Chinese restaurant. That night, I fell asleep to a public television pledge-a-thon offering a four-box-set collection of Peter, Paul and Mary's greatest hits. I awoke the next day to the smell of diesel from idling cars and the high-pitched voices of early morning day laborers. Going about my morning routine of yoga and meditation, I was grateful for the unhurried pace the day brought. Typically, I would have been out the door on my way to a long and stressful day working as a lawyer-lobbyist, putting out fires. But this day, I was in leisure, in retreat mode. After I ate breakfast and packed, my Haitian cab driver took me up the winding dirt road lined with dry grass of Melru Lane to the gates of Deer Park Monastery, which welcomed me with the message: "You have arrived."

I arrived at the Colors of Compassion Retreat feeling newish and inexperienced, though I had been ordained into the Order of Interbeing in August 2003 at Stonehill College, where I was given the Dharma name True Power of the Sangha (later changed to True Sangha Power, as mentioned in the Introduction.) I still recall my anticipation as the car wound up the dusty desert hill, not knowing what to expect, and feeling full of excitement about the first BIPOC retreat in the Plum Village community. When the car reached the top of the hill and the entrance to the monastery, I was amazed by the array of BIPOC. Some were dressed in traditional African clothing; others wore dashikis; and still others dressed in restrained Buddhist monastic robes. They all looked perfectly at home. They all belonged.

The retreat brought together over three hundred people of Asian American, Pacific Islander, African American, Latinx, Native American, Southwest Asian, and North African descent, and a few European American family members. Many were new to Buddhism; many were attending a retreat for the first time. Many were lesbian, gay, transgender, or bisexual. Organized in part through the dedication and vision of highly respected Black practitioners, Rev. Dr. Larry Ward and Kaira Jewel Lingo, a Black nun in the Plum Village tradition, this was, and still remains, the largest Buddhist retreat for people of color in North American history. The retreat was so inspirational that it led Thích Nhất Hạnh and Plum Village to commit to offering more of those types of retreats. It spawned a movie entitled *Colors of Compassion* and a book titled *Together We Are One: Honoring Our Diversity, Celebrating Our Connection*. Today, some sanghas worldwide support BIPOC, Muslim, LGBTQIA+, disabled, and other marginalized groups, thanks to this retreat and all its fruits.

Twenty years later, as I walked to the altar with Brother Pháp Dung to offer a Dharma talk on the third day of the historic anniversary retreat, I felt the poignancy of the moment. Looking out onto the sea of faces in a kaleidoscope of colors, I thought about Thầy and his beautiful legacy of engaged social action, his teaching that we exist in a profound state of interconnectedness and interdependence, or interbeing, and his urgent message of mindfulness, concentration, and insight. Perhaps most of all, I thought about belonging and connectedness.

In the late 1990s and early 2000s, when I started attending Plum Village retreats, I was filled with rage, hostility, and aggression, in part driven by my work as a lobbyist-lawyer, and partly fueled by experiences of being "othered," being "the only one," "one of few" people of color, or worse, experiences of outright racial hostility. Gradually and with the support of the sangha, I transformed these feelings by calming my nervous system, reflecting on my life with the support of the sangha, supportive family and friends, and therapy, understanding what happened to me and why, and practicing mindfulness in daily life.

Twenty years ago, attendees at Plum Village retreats were almost entirely white. I was often one of the only BIPOC participants, or one of very few present. I felt like an anomaly, like I didn't belong. Sometimes retreatants would ask me questions like, "What are you doing here?" or "Why do you stay?" Some of these questions were rooted in genuine curiosity, but they only amplified my sense of isolation as a Black woman in a predominantly white space. I realized, too, that many BIPOC participants who attended these early retreats shared similar experiences of feeling unsafe, or feeling that they didn't belong. Many didn't return.

Despite the challenges, I stayed. The practice benefited me profoundly. I had to unlearn harmful patterns and beliefs, and I am deeply grateful for the community that supported my transformation. Early on, I found connection with other Black practitioners (Kaira Jewel Lingo and Larry Ward, specifically), but the experience was still isolating. Looking back, I see that the environment—while rooted in love, compassion, and service—wasn't fully equipped to address the unique needs of BIPOC practitioners. We bring with us our inherited social conditioning and the habit energies of our experiences, as well as societal legacy burdens of prejudice, oppression, discrimination, and more. When these realities go unacknowledged, they can create barriers, even in a space as loving as a Plum Village retreat.

Today, the landscape is different. There is a collective effort to increase diversity and create spaces where BIPOC and other practitioners feel welcomed and supported. Groups like the ARISE Sangha and initiatives for BIPOC Dharma Sharing have flourished. Non-BIPOC practitioners have also engaged in deeper self-reflection, especially in recent years after the murder of George Floyd in 2020 and the movement to protect Black lives.

Yet, there's still much work to do. As of this writing, BIPOC representation in teaching roles and among attendees remains unbalanced, both at Plum Village and in Buddhist centers across North America. Addressing these disparities is vital for the sangha's growth and health and to create true happiness rooted in belonging and inclusiveness for everyone.

Contemplation on the Third Mindfulness Training

Cherishment as True Love

Aware of the suffering caused by discrimination and oppression, I vow to transform these seeds in myself, my sangha, and society. I recognize the ways in which I have benefitted or not benefitted, explicitly or implicitly, from systems and structures of injustice. I am aware of the legacy of violence, including unlawful police violence, perpetrated against people of various gender identities, expressions, and sexual orientations, Black people, indigenous people, people of color, people with disabilities, undocumented people, people suffering mental health challenges, and others who are marginalized. I am committed to looking tenderly at my suffering, knowing that I am not separate from others and that the seeds of suffering contain the seeds of joy. I am aware that narrow interpretations of intimate relationships constrain how we cherish each other in our expression of love, leaving many isolated and alienated. I am not afraid of bold love that fosters compassion, justice, and peace, and tender love that seeks understanding. I cherish this breath, body, mind, and moment as an act of healing for myself and for others. I cherish the liberation of all beings guided by the wisdom and the solidity of the sangha as my path of true love.

Marisela:

This Contemplation continues to grow my love and reverence for my life. It is an example of how the Trainings and Contemplations truly rest on and help each other become realized. As I continue to cherish and value myself, and as I release and put down the stories of being inferior, insufficient, or not smart enough, I become more rooted into solidity, more steady, and braver. It is important to say that even after obtaining multiple degrees, my inferiority complex was still very present from the pernicious social conditioning of being in this human form. Through the practice of grounding myself in the earth and reconnecting with the power of the elements, I came to understand that I am no less powerful than these elements in and around me. Therefore, I am no less or more than all other beings made from these same elements.

As this transformation occurs, courage grows enough for me to delve into the traumas and sufferings that have kept me contracted and knotted up, taking up space and creating a tight net, a lattice that has not allowed me the spaciousness to reveal my most true self. In order to cherish myself, I give myself the time needed to take good care: I take breaks not just when needed but also scheduled into my day as preventative medicine. When I schedule breaks during the day, the week, and so on, it helps keep me on the path of caring for myself. After many years of pushing hard and getting things accomplished, I realized that a certain degree of ignoring care for myself had to occur in order to keep pushing. As the distracted mind is cloudy and full, how could it not ignore certain needs? This had become normalized for me, and sometimes it's still easy to revert back into this mode. When I am tired, it is easier to revert to old ways of putting the needs of others before my own, like staying up late to reach a timeline. When I am relaxed and rested, valuing and loving myself is much easier because there is more clarity.

Cherishing myself also may sometimes look like saying no to someone else. This used to be hard to do. Now my yes to someone else is also a yes to myself instead of a no to myself. Cherishing myself is listening deeply to myself, as instructed in the Fourth Mindfulness Training and Contemplation. This listening allows me to recognize what is truly needed in the moment. Caring for myself ultimately allows me to care for others from a heart of fullness and true generosity without expecting anything in return. With such wholesome fullness and contentment, there is no need to receive more, and there is less inner chatter instructing me that I need more conditions to be happy.

Technology is an external chatter that stimulates and adds to the inner chatter. In this age of nonstop growth, it is challenging to not become caught up in the toxicity of technology consumption. Because technology has increased the rate of everything, without mindfulness of how we use our devices it is easy to be taken in by the "urgency" of someone's communication. The introduction of electronic mail (email) in the early 1990s for work purposes created a new expectation for how quickly we should engage with work communications; gradually, work emails began taking up our personal time. Email slowly spread as a general mode of communication and continued to take us away from ourselves—from just sitting still and gazing at a plant, or engaging in exercise or a kind act, or simply not having to consume another thing. Then came texting on mobile phones. Initially, texting on phones was more or less for personal use, and it was another thing that stole our time away from cherishing ourselves through giving attention to ourselves. Slowly, it became more "convenient" for many to use phone texting in the process of work. One of my practices for "taking care of me time" is to refrain from doing work through phone texting. When others attempt to pull me into text-work, I gently request that work matters stay on email. I also attempt to check emails only two times daily, and I seldom respond to an email the first time I read it. These small acts of protecting my time feel like ways to cherish myself as I acknowledge that stillness and noise-free environments help me to reset and relax my nervous system, which allows me to notice my mind and heart and body. I also try to offer this same respect and cherishment for others by not expecting quick responses to the electronic communications I send. Taking this time for myself and others feels like an attempt to reset expectations around creating a culture of urgency, which is toxic to our nervous system, clouds our thoughts, and causes us to lose our ability to be in the present moment.

Cherishing myself is a moment-by-moment practice. It is an undoing of not only my lifetime, but also of the lifetimes of all the ancestors in me who were demonized and marginalized for who they were. In the United States, daily, we breathe an air that normalizes the enforcement of American global sovereignty and a steady stream of violence against marginalized people. The current government's inhumane mass deportation of immigrants, toxic masculinity and misogyny, disregard of the genocidal history and legacy of African enslavement, continued land and water extraction from Indigenous people, and indirect and direct support of genocide against the Palestinian state, are watering in me the seeds of a misperception that "there is something wrong with you and people like you." Cherishing myself sits in the middle of the Contemplations on the Five Mindfulness Trainings to assure that I have reverence for and welcome my life and the lives of others like me, that I stay connected and vulnerable, and that I feel like I belong and am valued. When I can practice like this, it naturally opens me up to do the same with all beings, regardless of socially constructed identities.

Valerie:
Growing a garden is a living act of love, hope, and potential. A garden cannot be planted without these essentials. They are as elemental as soil, air, and water for the garden to grow.

I became a gardener after having lost sight of these essentials of love, hope, and potential. I was buried beneath the rubble of a life of too much toughness and not enough tenderness. My love for growing things began decades ago, even before I moved to Bucks County and my tiny plot of lawn, in northern New Mexico, where I worked as a farmhand at an experimental research farm in the high desert. I planted forty pounds of garlic, one clove at a time, in the shadow of mesas, pastel-colored canyons, cliffs, plains, grasslands, and streams. I fell deeply in love with the desert soil, air, water, and sky. It was there that I began to realize that to grow a garden, to plant a clove of garlic, or a seed, or a tree, is the living theology of love. It is to water seeds of love, peace, and compassion.

Many years ago, when I arrived in New Mexico from Brooklyn, I realized that I was starved for beauty, or at the very least, I couldn't see the beauty that surrounded me. I'd spent much of my life trying to make myself into something and someone. I had run from Brooklyn to undergrad school, grad school, law school, and then to the big and important job as a lawyer-lobbyist. There was just one problem: the job was killing my spirit and my soul. A turning point came while I was on vacation in the high desert of New Mexico. I climbed to the top of a big hill. I took off my backpack, sat with my back against a nurse log, and looked up at the big sky. For the first time, I truly noticed; I saw the clouds. I saw the blue sky.

I noticed how the clouds moved. In that stunning moment, I realized that I was alienated not only from the natural world but also from myself. Decades of trying to assimilate as a Black woman into white dominant culture left me alienated from myself, from my body, from deeper relationships, and from the natural world.

The First Foundation of Mindfulness is awareness of the body. Mindful awareness invites the practitioner to see, touch, taste, and smell, to be fully alive in the present moment, alive to the great gift of life. Mindfulness is an innate quality in every person that supports awakening to the unique nature of each and every moment of daily life. Gardening became a theology of love that invited me back to my senses, which were deadened by too-muchness, too-soonness, and too-fastness. Gradually, with the support of the Plum Village community, I began to look tenderly at my suffering, knowing that I was not separate from others and that the seeds of suffering contained the seeds of joy.

My healing was deeply connected to planting and gardening. I started dreaming about the garden I would plant when Peter, my husband, and I moved into my barn-house outside of Philadelphia. Over the years, the marriage was choked out by sadness, isolation, and an ambiguous love. He moved out during an excessive heat warning in July, and as he drove away my heart shattered again into a million pieces, activating the seed-like emotions of shame, despair, and isolation. Looking back now, I see that this was a necessary ending laden with potential, much like the garden in my dreams. As a lawyer, I knew nothing about compassionate listening and loving speech. I had a well-tended adversarial mindset that contributed to the ending of our marriage. In other words, the basis for true love wasn't there; I craved control in the marriage as a way of compensating for other aspects of my life that I felt were beyond my control. I lacked the skill or understanding to support a trusting and loving relationship, and to be honest, so did Peter. Families and friends could feel and sense our despair and stayed clear of us. I was a Dharmacharya at the time and, as the marriage was coming apart, a nagging voice in the back of my head was saying: *Dharma teachers don't get divorced. They live happy, contented, well-rounded family lives.*

With all this, I set out to reclaim my inner gardener, to water the seeds of peace, understanding, and love within me. I replaced rotten wood and painted my barn-house. I removed diseased trees that threatened to fall on the house and heaps of junk, replaced the cottage roof, and painted over graffiti. Then I turned to a small koi pond that had been a source of joy but over the years, like the marriage, had stagnated with standing muddy water, overgrown cattails, and arrowheads, empty of fish. Shovel by shovel, I worked with a couple friends and helpers to move plants and rocks, remove overgrown weeds, and reclaim the soil with organic matter.

Each month brought a new challenge in the garden: groundhogs, carpenter bees, wasps, and hard-as-rocks clay soil. While the garden was being reborn, my brother was dying. He died in February of 2020, and this was followed by desperate months of quarantine, isolation, and physical distance, as well as the disproportionate impact of COVID-19 on the most vulnerable people, the unlawful police killing of George Floyd and others, and the racial reckoning worldwide as protesters called to defund police, sparked by the Black Lives Matter movement.

It was a sunny day in July, and I had been living unpartnered for nearly one year. I walked outside and looked at the place that had been a hole in the ground with stagnant water. Now in its place was the sound of water from a glazed fountain, hummingbirds, butterflies, and goldfinches at my Nyjer seed feeder. There was pink *Echinacea purpurea,* feathery white *Artemisia schmidtiana*, vivid red *Crocosmia* hybrid, and lemon yellow *Coreopsis verticillata*. I went over to the giant staghorn fern and took it down to give it a good watering. Days earlier, I had noticed that a tiny song sparrow built a nest of pine needles behind the plant. As I put the nozzle deep into the cavity of the fern, I stopped. There, huddled together, lay five tiny brown speckled eggs.

In the Plum Village tradition, we are invited to wake up to suffering within and around us and hold it with care, to get to know suffering, and to transform it into compassion, peace, and love. We are invited to cultivate a safe haven with each breath, for ourselves and for all living beings. The making of this garden taught me to dig deep, deeper still, and to know that love is a digger.

Contemplation on the Fourth Mindfulness Training

Vulnerability as Deep Listening and Loving Speech

Aware that vulnerability is the essence of our true nature, our humanness, I vow to risk listening for understanding rather than disagreement. I am committed to generous and courageous listening that bridges differences and supports others who may be different from me. When I am not able to understand others, I vow to come back to my breath and my body, and to offer myself gentle patience. I am aware that loving communication rests on honesty, compassion, and openness that align with my highest aspiration to alleviate suffering. When I have hurt others through my unskillful listening or speech, I vow to practice true beneficial regret, making a good apology that acknowledges what I have done and the harm caused, accepting responsibility and being accountable for my behavior, and offering sincere regret for my actions, knowing that this supports the other person and me. Through my practices of vulnerability, forgiveness, and deep listening, I know that my speech will be guided by love and understanding. Practicing in this way supports Right Speech and Right Action and guides me to Right Insight.

Marisela:

This Contemplation reminds me that I have a choice in how I show up, and that it matters. I can choose to close off my heart or I can choose to slowly open my heart in listening and communicating. When I practice with an open heart, it helps others around me also open their hearts. The energy my speech brings is directly related to how my heart feels. The energy I offer in listening is also determined by the status of my heart. I find that being intentional in my speech or listening requires me to be fully present. Breathing and coming back to my body helps me to be fully present. I begin to notice what is alive in me at the moment, and I make a conscious decision to show up in love.

Listening and speaking from a vulnerable or open heart is crucial in moments of chaos. At a recent rally for peace in Palestine, offering a guided meditation from a big heart was important. I couldn't wait until I was home in a quiet space with a candle and sage. My heart needed to be open right there, not constricted from anger because of the genocide being supported by the US. I find that to love is to be vulnerable. In moments of chaos, I still want to love, which means I must stay open. In light of this, I find myself happy to be alive at a time when the United States is being governed by an authoritarian regime. It is critical to show up vulnerable at times when we might close our hearts off in fear. It is natural for us to respond to unknowns with fear, anger, sadness, or frustration, especially in situations of harm or potential harm. Yet more and more, I see how important it is to maintain some form of openness, even in these moments. If I contract and close down, my new fear (or anger, or sadness, etc.) cannot become transformed in that moment. It becomes stuck in me and this is where it will stay, and this new trauma will create its own world inside me. It will find other traumas stuck in me and continue to grow a bigger world of traumas inside me, covering up my true self. Listening and speaking from a space of vulnerability, with an energy that is moving toward spaciousness, allows this new energy that is manifesting as grief or frustration to go through me in this new moment and not build on the old traumas.

Being openhearted allows me to be welcoming and connecting, not individualistic, fearful, righteous, and cold. Openheartedness is an energy that welcomes instead of shuts down, and it offers potential for collective transformation. Being mindful that I choose to show up with the energy of vulnerability requires that I continuously listen to myself, including my self-talk. How does my self-talk build spaciousness inside? What am I saying to myself when I make mistakes? Am I repeating old chatter, like "You're not enough" and "You don't belong"? Or is my self-talk kind and reverent? Am I watering my seeds of openness? Rebuilding this self to be more open and connecting within myself translates to the same openness toward people and situations outside of me. When I am aware that it all begins and ends with me, that everything is first created in the mind, my mind, I become more careful in how I talk and act toward myself. I attempt to let go of the restrictions that prevent the energy of spaciousness from manifesting. As spacious energy manifests, my inner and outer communication becomes a sign of my path of freedom. Each moment of freedom allows the possibility of another moment of freedom. My thoughts, speech, and action are continuously in awareness on this path of freedom as I strive to offer vulnerability to myself and the world. In these times of chaos, I am even more aware that if I shut down, I cannot listen fully. And listening deeply requires me to stay soft inside. Staying soft inside seems to translate to staying soft outside as well.

Valerie:

As a lawyer, I was trained in law school to listen with a critical ear and to listen for disagreement. I filtered what I heard through this lens and then seized the moment to convince the other person of my rightness. Being The Big Shot Lawyer, I had the answer before the question was asked. My habit of listening and speaking was to give unsolicited quick-fix solutions, cut people off, become easily bored, deflect sincere compliments to avoid connection, or jump to conclusions. This way of listening wrecked two marriages. The truth is that underneath this destructive pattern was a fear of being vulnerable, of risking showing my true feelings or making authentic contact that might signal my needs.

This pattern, especially deflecting connection, persisted not just in my marriage but in nearly all my communications. I recall a very ordinary conversation with my niece, Joanne. One day while she was visiting me, she offered me a sincere compliment. True to form, I deflected it. Joanne stopped and said, "I notice that whenever I offer you a sincere compliment, you can't seem to accept it." I responded by brushing off her words, again deflecting. But in that moment, I realized Joanne was right and this pattern was a way of avoiding real intimacy, vulnerability, and connection. My behavior was driven, at least in part, by my personal history of discrimination, oppression, and feeling powerless or underestimating my own agency. That moment was a wake-up bell.

Today, I understand that the nature of connecting with myself and with others is an act of vulnerability, of risking openness and honesty. Coming to this understanding of how to truly connect and communicate with another person has taken many years, and I wrecked two marriages in the process of learning. One insight from my learning is that one of the most important ways I can connect with another person is to confirm and validate them and what they are saying. It is powerful to confirm and validate another person by saying things like: "That makes sense." "I can see how you might feel that way." "Tell me more about… " Confirming and validating is not the same as agreeing. I can disagree with the content but still validate the person's lived experience. I am not trying to "fix" or "solve" their problem. I am not offering unsolicited opinions or advice, which can sometimes shift the focus toward myself and away from the person who is suffering. I remember that the person is whole, creative, and resourceful, and has agency, capacity, and choice. Offering genuine attentiveness and validation goes a long way in creating emotional attunement, connection, and support.

In listening, I keep the focus on supporting the other person by hearing not just what is said but also what is *unsaid*, or the emotions below the words. Offering validation goes deeper than hearing the words; instead, it goes to the feelings. This is turning toward and joining with, even when there is disagreement. When we confirm and validate the perspective of another person, even if we don't agree with them—and especially with people who are very different from us—we make space for complicated emotions. We recognize the universal quality of our shared humanity. We stand *with* rather than stand apart from the other. We meet each other in our mutual fragility and mutual resilience.

An important aspect of this way of connecting with another is the practice of bearing witness. I am thinking of the work of Roshi Bernie Glassman and the Zen Peacemakers. The practice of bearing witness is to see all, and not to turn away from difficult aspects of a situation, including one's own beliefs, attachments, and judgments. When you bear witness, you allow yourself to meet whatever is arising and become acquainted with it just as it is. When combined with the Buddhist practice of a nonjudgmental, open mindset and awareness, bearing witness can strengthen your capacity to be a nonreactive, spacious presence. It can strengthen your capacity to listen to another's suffering without the urge to "fix it," give unsolicited advice, disappear, minimize, or bypass. Whatever emerges is held in the light of tender witnessing.

Contemplation on the Fifth Mindfulness Training

Welcoming as True Nourishing and Healing

Aware of the suffering caused by the consumption of an inadequate history of racial and ethnic forms of social segregation and injustice, I am committed to healing myself and the world. I am aware that my thoughts, perceptions, feelings, words, and actions may have been influenced by this history. I vow to understand how I have been influenced by embracing and denying this racial, social, and ethnic history of inferiority, superiority, and equality. I will cultivate joy to nourish me in this aspiration. I will practice mindfulness of the Four Kinds of Nutriments to become aware of how edible foods, sense impressions, volition, and consciousness are all influenced by this history. Practicing with Right Energy and Right Resolve, my conscious consumption will be guided by Right Action that welcomes differences without discrimination. This Right Insight offers true welcoming on this path to nourish and heal myself, my ancestors, my descendants, my sangha, and society.

Marisela:

This Contemplation reminds me to welcome all parts of me. In the past, it was difficult to be present for the parts of me that felt hurt or ashamed. The parts that are tied up in knots, holding tension in my body and mind, have old narratives that require listening with care. Each story I have consumed that says, "You are inferior, you are not enough," must be unpacked. For example, the story "Sexually abused people invited their abuse" stayed with me for a long time. As I began to look deeply into this often false narrative, I began to see that its messaging was also fed by a fragile child who already felt inferior. Abuse simply nourished that existing inferiority complex. Each of these stories has a resting place in me, an imprint that wants to be tended to, cared for, and transformed. When they are uncared for or unwelcomed, they present themselves in other ways, as unwholesome mental formations: anger, sadness, despair, impatience, jealousy, revenge, etc. Welcoming and transforming these imprints is like taking their nourishment away—it leaves no fuel for the unwholesomeness to manifest. Without nourishment from stuck tensions, the mental formations grow smaller and smaller. Welcoming the imprints with compassion leads to care and transformation; then love and understanding grow larger, revealing and providing nourishment for continued healing to occur.

Recently I have been practicing with welcoming aspects of me that historically I had not identified as "me." It's a simple practice, but it has slowly opened me up to accepting everything in me. It's a bit like the way Christian mystics speak about God welcoming all God's children, no matter what they have done. It started with the colors of clothing I wear. Historically I wouldn't wear pastel colors. My mom gave me some pastel tops and I told her, "You know I don't wear those types of colors." Then I reflected on this because she had taken her time to choose them for me and I wanted to show appreciation. Curiously, once I wore a light green top, the rigidity of "This is not my color" immediately fell away. It was as if I stepped out of a duality of "bold versus pastel" and into a realm of "What's the difference?" It opened a door to welcoming all colors, literally. Nothing was off limits. This was a small shift in one of the defining perceptions of who I thought I was.

This small shift made me question all the perceptions I had of myself, especially the ones that had bolder colors, meaning they were more saturated, bolder perceptions of myself. "More saturated" translates into "harder" or "bolder" in the ways I have shown up. We can link this to "less feminine" if we categorize it by the historical narrative of masculine and feminine dualities and the characteristics we ascribe to them. "Harder" or "bolder" can be translated as being more likely to name something that is perceived as problematic and being more direct in the way I communicate and address others. Welcoming the thought that I didn't have to only show up like this was a taste of freedom—there is no certainty in defining myself, and all aspects are welcome. It also led me to look more deeply into why I have shown up in this way. We tend to believe that our ways of being, our characteristics, define us:

"This is who I am." Looking at my life experiences as a Black-Brown, female-bodied, queer immigrant from a working-class background, I see that I have had my fair share of oppressive interactions that landed as unjust and needing correction. In the past, not once would I consider that perhaps "I" didn't need to be the one to correct them. In fact, it felt like I needed to be the one to correct my injustices and the injustices of all people who suffered similarly or suffered any oppression. But is that a Right View? Knowing suffering does not mean one has to be the person who always seeks to bring sufficient conditions for transformation of its causes and conditions.

Mindfulness allows me to reconsider, in stillness, what is happening in me. What is getting nourished right now? What is there that is making me react or respond in this way? Can I acknowledge and embrace it? Can I be kind to myself? Can I cherish all of me, the pain, the traumas, the beauty, and the transformations? This is true welcoming: turning to and welcoming all that is there, noting what has been fed and allowed to grow, choosing what to continue to grow, and being aware of what is needing transformation. Welcoming allows me to move from the dualistic notions of right and wrong, good and bad. It allows me to recognize that there is no permanent self of Marisela but instead a form that is made up of many different experiences and interactions. Therefore, I will continue to be made up of future experiences and interactions. To the extent that I can choose and welcome the more wholesome experiences, I can also choose to continue evolving in my path of awakening into right understanding.

Valerie:

Healing is not linear but instead is a process of gradually acknowledging, understanding, and transforming our thoughts, perceptions, feelings, and actions.

Over many years, I have offered facilitation in all types of retreats. In BIPOC retreats, especially, I have found that many people arrive seeking a place of refuge and safety, having carried for a lifetime the burdens of discrimination, marginalization, and oppression, and an accompanying sense of heightened vigilance.

Several years ago, I experienced a powerful reminder of these burdens when I facilitated an online BIPOC mindfulness retreat focused on healing. One participant, a Black woman living in a high-rise building in Chicago, shared that she never left her apartment without carrying her wallet containing her ID and her phone—not even when she took out the trash. She lived in a constant state of fear, always bracing herself, always vigilant for potential harm because of her identity as a Black person.

Throughout the retreat, she engaged deeply with the practices of mindful sitting, mindful walking, and mindful breathing. These practices, combined with the collective energy of the BIPOC sangha, helped her connect with a sense of safety she hadn't known before. By the end of the three-day retreat, she emailed me to share something extraordinary: for the first time in her life, she left her apartment without her wallet or phone. To many, this might seem like a small act, but for her, it was monumental. It represented a shift from living in constant vigilance to experiencing a moment of safety, healing, and ease. This transformation speaks to the profound power of a Beloved Community where people feel safe, supported, and seen, and where all are welcome. It is a testament to the Plum Village model of healing and transformation to which Thầy dedicated his life, and to the strength of collective healing and the impact of creating spaces where BIPOC people can feel at ease and be fully present.

Moments like these are why BIPOC retreats and other affinity group retreats matter. They offer sanctuary, a space where individuals can touch a sense of freedom and peace, even in a world that often denies them these experiences. This woman's story is one of many, and it reminds me of the transformative potential of this practice when paired with the support of a loving and inclusive community.

4

Practicing the Five Mindfulness Trainings and Contemplations Together

While reading and studying the Trainings and Contemplations can help us name a path of ethical conduct and wisdom and point us in the direction of that path, we must practice and apply them to fully experience the benefit.

The Five Mindfulness Trainings invite you to become aware of your thoughts, feelings, and actions, your immediate surroundings, and your larger environment. Thầy says that in considering these precepts for daily living, you should also consider practice (*sila*) of the precepts, concentration (*samadhi*), and insight (*prajna*)—the Threefold Training. The precepts, concentration, and insight are interconnected: Practicing the precepts gives rise to mindfulness. Concentration is an aspect of mindfulness that allows you to look deeply into something specific in your life, to explore, reflect, consider, and ponder. Insight is the fruit of looking deeply.[22] The insight that emerges from practicing with the precepts grows from your lived experience, from what you have actually observed and realized. In other words, you study the precepts and then apply them to your daily life through practice, which supports your understanding and insight. Wisdom is born out of your own practice, concentration, and insight.

With this in mind, we provide the following exercises and inquiries for you to practice and reflect on. Notice for yourself what arises. You might like to keep a record, noting what you discover before, during, and after you practice with these inquiries in a journal. Feel welcome to practice with these inquiries in buddy groups or sanghas. You might like to practice with one of these inquiries for a week or two before moving on to another; there is no set order to follow other than what feels truly helpful.

Reflection Practices

Before reflecting on any of the Trainings or Contemplations, establish yourself in mindfulness by practicing with awareness of breath, body, or sound for three to five minutes. You might like to have a small bell to invite at the beginning of this awareness practice and at the end of the inquiry and reflective practice. Read or speak out loud the Five Mindfulness Trainings and Contemplations from this book or from another source.

If you are practicing in a buddy group or sangha, you may like to hold space for any noticings or discoveries you feel comfortable sharing before closing the group with three sounds of the bell.

Mindfulness of Breath, Body, and Sound

Breathing in, wake up the bell by using the inviter (the stick) to gently sound the bell by resting the inviter firmly on the side of the bell and leaving it there to soften the resonance. Then invite three full sounds of the bell, allowing the resonance of each sound to trail off before inviting the next sound.

> ***Mindfulness of Breath:*** *Breathing in and out in awareness, become aware of your breath entering your body and leaving your body. Notice the length and depth of the breath.*
>
> ***Mindfulness of Body:*** *Breathing in, notice your body in space, the touch points against surfaces that support you. Notice what is there in the body without judgment.*
>
> ***Mindfulness of Sound:*** *Breathing in, begin to notice external sounds in your environment. Be curious about the sounds. Bring your awareness to the sounds of your breath entering and leaving the body, the heartbeat, the pulse.*

The First Mindfulness Training: Reverence for Life

Gently breathe into your heart space with love and kindness. Reflect on an aspect of yourself that you may not hold in reverence. (For example, you might reflect on a tendency to react quickly in anger.) Bring this part of yourself into your heart space and send it love and kindness. Tell this part of yourself that you want to understand it better and are open to listening. Rest your awareness in your heart space for a few minutes. Note what arises after this practice.

Contemplation on the First Mindfulness Training: Acknowledging Beauty as Reverence for Life

Gently breathe into your heart space with love and kindness, acknowledging that we are inherently beautiful. Reflect on an aspect of yourself that you think is ugly or unattractive. (For example, you might reflect on the size or shape of a particular body part.) Bring your awareness to this aspect of yourself, and send it love and kindness. Note the energy that arises when you do this. Tell this part of yourself that it is sufficient, beautiful, perfect as it is, and loved. Notice any changes in the energy in this part of your body. Stay with this reflection for a few minutes. Note what arises after this practice.

Invite yourself to contemplate the First Mindfulness Training, Reverence for Life, and feel free to write your own contemplation.

The Second Mindfulness Training: True Happiness

Remember a time, a place, or an occasion when you felt a deep happiness. Notice if there is a particular part of your body that resonates with this thought. From this area of your body, let the energetic sensation, shape, vibration, odor, or color slowly begin to move through your entire body. Notice if an energy of happiness has grown in the original area of your body. Recognize whether there is any increase or decrease here when this energy is shared with the rest of the body. After a few moments, open your eyes and record any noticings or discoveries.

Contemplation on the Second Mindfulness Training: Belonging and Connecting as True Happiness

Bring into mind an occasion when you felt you belonged, or a place or people with whom you felt you belonged. Notice in your body where there might be resonance with this feeling of belonging. Bring to mind an occasion when you felt you did not belong. Notice in your body where this might resonate, and allow your awareness to go to the area of your body feeling belonging. Begin to slowly breathe the sensations of belonging into the areas of non-belonging by connecting them. Notice how easy or difficult it is to connect these areas. If any judgment arises, simply put it aside and return to sharing the energies of belonging with the areas of non-belonging. After a few minutes, open your eyes and notice what is there in mind and body.

Invite yourself to contemplate the Second Mindfulness Training, True Happiness, and feel free to write your own contemplation.

The Third Mindfulness Training: True Love

Consider these questions: What does true love mean to you? What spiritual support have you cultivated in the form of family, friends, mentors, and others?

Contemplation on the Third Mindfulness Training: Cherishment as True Love

Bring to mind a behavior you cherish about yourself. The energy of "not allowing" is powerful and may defeat the intent and efficacy of this practice: Can you stay with this and not allow other thoughts to minimize it? Notice any place in the body where this resonates. Notice the sensations here, and slowly let them spread throughout the body. Allow your entire body to feel and to receive this energy of cherishment. Stay with this for a few minutes, noting if there is any particular area where it may be more difficult to spread this energy. After a few minutes, open your eyes and record any noticings.

Invite yourself to contemplate the Third Mindfulness Training, True Love, and feel free to write your own contemplation.

The Fourth Mindfulness Training: Loving Speech and Deep Listening

How have your perceptions influenced your thinking, your actions, your feelings, and your moods?

What do you notice about your habits and practices in listening to others and to yourself?

When you listen to another person, focus on practicing listening in a way that helps them to transform suffering and "see a way out of difficult situations." Notice what happens.

Contemplation on the Fourth Mindfulness Training: Vulnerability as Deep Listening and Loving Speech

What is the connection between vulnerability and listening for understanding? How do you offer forgiveness and grace to yourself and others? The next time you have a disagreement with another person, practice making a "good apology" and offering "sincere beneficial regret." Notice what arises.

Invite yourself to contemplate the Fourth Mindfulness Training, Loving Speech and Deep Listening, and feel free to write your own contemplation.

The Fifth Mindfulness Training: Nourishment and Healing

What do you consume on a daily basis? What do you notice about how and what you consume on a daily basis and the effects on you, others around you, and our broader society? The next time you purchase an item from a grocery store, consider where it comes from and where it will go after you use it. What information is there for you? What action will you take as a result of this knowledge?

Contemplation on the Fifth Mindfulness Training: Welcoming as True Nourishing and Healing

How have you learned about the history of racial and ethnic forms of social segregation? In what ways have you been influenced by embracing and denying the racial, social, and ethnic history of inferiority, superiority, and equality?

Invite yourself to contemplate the Fifth Mindfulness Training, Nourishment and Healing, and feel free to write your own contemplation.

Choose a practice that brings you joy (for example, being in nature, feeling your breath in the moment, offering support to another) to cultivate and nourish your aspiration to heal yourself, others, and our society. After one week of practicing daily, notice any shifts in your way of thinking and acting. Don't feel pressured if you don't notice anything. Simply continue to practice daily and notice each week any changes. Your explorations will encourage you to regularly schedule time for practicing in these ways.

Creating Your Own Contemplations

After some time practicing with the Trainings and these Contemplations, you may like to write your own contemplations, bringing your lived experience directly into the Mindfulness Trainings. Gather something to write with and some paper or a journal. Instead of writing, you may wish to move your body or create a gesture, sing, draw, paint, knit, sculpt, or otherwise craft or create your own contemplations in an expressive way that nourishes you.

Sit quietly for a few minutes, coming back to your body, coming back to your breath. Choose which Mindfulness Training you would like to contemplate and read it slowly, either to yourself or out loud. Reflect quietly for one to two minutes, then read it again—maybe this time out loud, if you read it silently to yourself the first time. Reflect for a few minutes. Read a third time. Allow yourself to absorb the Training and notice what arises for you. Take your time writing what came up; this can be one sentence or several. You can also try drawing or moving your body. Allow your heart to connect to what you create, without judgment or filters. Enjoy the process as you embody the Training and integrate it with your life experience, reflected in your contemplative process.

This practice can also be done with a friend or in a group. A facilitator can invite the group into this same process, and each person practices creating their own contemplation. In a group setting, the facilitator can also invite one or two people to share their creation with the group. Gathering together in this way invites us to deepen our friendships and connect with others to cocreate contemplative and peaceful lives together as a liberatory practice.

Through contemplating the Five Mindfulness Trainings in these ways, the values you hold most dear become alive in you. We hope these reflective practices help you develop a living relationship to the ethical framework of the Five Mindfulness Trainings, so that the teachings themselves feel like friends. Having these spiritual friends to guide us is a gift. When Ananda, the Buddha's attendant, mused that having good friends and companions are half of the spiritual life, the Buddha gently corrected him: such friends are the whole of the spiritual life; the spiritual friendship *is the whole path of liberation.*[23] We trust that your earnest practice with the Five Mindfulness Trainings will support your deepest aspirations, protect you from what can be a brutal social environment, and, right in the midst of our world's anger, pain, rage, sadness, grief, and impatience, help you find beauty, joy, friendship, love, and liberation.

Chapter 5

Five Practitioners Offer Reflections on Living the Five Mindfulness Trainings and Contemplations

Reflections on the First Mindfulness Training and Contemplation: Finding Wholeness and a Journey Through Violence, Healing, and Joy

Name: Hawah Bunduka/Gentle Manifestation of the Source
Pronouns: she/her
Location: Barcelona, Spain

I grew up in a household marked by domestic violence. My mother eventually found the strength to break free, but the years of witnessing and enduring that environment left a deep imprint on me. I carry the effects of that trauma to this day and live with complex PTSD, which continues to shape the way I manage my emotions.

Entering my working life, I carried with me a strong awareness of the violence that exists in the world. That awareness fueled my drive to resist and fight against it. At the same time, the joyful and beautiful aspects of life—dance, carnival, music, and cultural expression—existed mostly on the margins as something I engaged in outside of work. These passions are deeply tied to my Sierra Leonean heritage, where dancing and celebration are part of who we are.

For a long time, I kept these two worlds separate. But over the last several years, I have begun to see the value of bringing them together. Rather than keeping joy and beauty apart from my professional life, I have learned to weave them into my work with survivors, marginalized groups, and people experiencing trauma. Through dance, mindfulness, and movement, I've cultivated balance, ensuring that my work is not consumed by despair but also nourished by joy.

This integration has extended into my personal and family life. As a mother, I've had to face how the violence I experienced growing up can show up in my own reactions, in moments of snapping or losing my temper. Acknowledging this has been part of my healing and growth. Instead of living fragmented lives—professional, personal, activist—I now seek wholeness, meshing these dimensions together.

When it comes to resistance, I have learned to choose my battles. I fight fiercely where it matters most—protecting my son from racism within the school system and society. In other areas, I've let go of the pressure to educate or save everyone. This shift has been essential for my well-being, helping me nurture myself and my child instead of burning out in constant struggle.

As a Black woman, a single mother, and the parent of a Black mixed-race child living in Spain, I know how easy it is to fall into being the "angry Black woman" at all times. For years, I embodied that role, justifiably so, but I now see how much it harmed me and impacted my son. Today, I practice discernment—resisting where necessary, but also stepping back, choosing silence, stillness, or reflection when that serves me better.

The practice of pausing—of noticing my emotions, my racing heart, my urge to react—has been transformative. With CPTSD, the instinct is often to be overly reactive, but I have become better at recognizing when I am in that mode and allowing myself to wait. Sometimes silence, or simply taking a breath, is the most powerful response.

These Contemplations and practices have offered me liberation: liberation from the isms and schisms of the world, and the freedom to be more of who I want to be. They remind me that all living beings have something to teach me. Even difficult relationships now hold lessons because they allow me to see myself in others and approach these difficulties with more compassion.

Finally, I hold a deep reverence for beauty. That is why I call our community the "Beautiful Sangha." As BIPOC—Black, Brown, and mixed people—our beauty is so often unrecognized or undervalued in mainstream culture, and even among ourselves. For me, beauty is not only about appearance but also about the resilience and grace of walking this path together, despite the oppression we face.

To gather in community, to affirm our inherent beauty while confronting systems that seek to diminish us, is itself an act of resistance and healing. It is a reminder that, even in the face of violence, we can cultivate joy, wholeness, and reverence for life.

Reflections on the Second Mindfulness Training and Contemplation: True Happiness and Remembering the Blessedness of Life As It Is

Name: Dancing Water/Loving Patient Lotus of the Heart/ True Virtuous Healing/Chân Đức Liệu
Pronouns: they/we
Location: Taiwan

My name is Dancing Water and my pronouns are they/we. These pronouns allow me to be inclusive of all people. I was raised in Sydney, Australia, and Hong Kong, where many ancestral home altars only honor male figures; female ancestors are often absent. The choice of my pronouns is to recognize the importance of all people, regardless of their gender.

Ethnically, I am Han Chinese, the dominant ethnic group in China. My grandparents fled China to Hong Kong around World War II. My parents went to study in Sydney as teenagers and started a family there. When I was a child, we went to Hong Kong, where I grew up, studied, and worked. Later, I also studied in the United Kingdom and worked in the United States. I now live in Taiwan. Currently, the majority of my time and energy is channeled into spiritual study and practice, the art of living, volunteering, and sangha building.

In Asia, many people view Buddhist precepts as prohibitory rules. In fact, in Chinese, the word *precepts* (戒) translates to rules that restrict and prohibit certain behaviors. For me, the Trainings are "guiding principles," as described in this book; they are not a set of strict rules but are more like an invitation and encouragement. Thầy named them "mindfulness trainings" (正念修習) as they are designed to be practiced, and in that practice is a quality of repetition and adjustment. In this part of the world, we often learn by repeating and memorizing passages and facts. Repetition in spiritual practice helps to deepen understanding, and eventually with enough practice and repetition, there is mastery and ease in the practice, and fuller integration into daily life. I'm remembering a brother sharing with me how he had practiced the ten mindful movements every day for many years. His depth, ease, joy, mastery, and attunement to details and nuances of the practice were quite apparent through his instructions and embodiment. I like to study the Fourteen Mindfulness Trainings to deepen my understanding of the Trainings, and I ask questions of myself and others, which diversifies ways of practice and application.

I have a particular interest in the Second Mindfulness Training, True Happiness (幸福). For me, this training is about contentment and blessedness more than happiness as an emotion. By contentment I mean recognition that I/we have enough, and that the circumstances in the present moment are enough and don't need to be any different for me/us to feel grateful, content, or blessed. Sometimes when life gets challenging, I imagine even more challenging circumstances, and I really ponder that possibility. And then I say to myself, "It could be worse… and it's not." I smile, and this shift in perspective helps me remember I already have so much. I have a renewed sense of gratitude and contentment for conditions as they exist now. True happiness (幸福) is about remembering the blessedness of life as it is and smiling with gratitude and contentment. I'm remembering a nine-year-old Iraqi girl I served. She had resettled in the United States as a refugee. She shared how she wasn't bothered by the children in school who made fun of her because it was "nothing" in contrast to almost being killed by the bombs falling on her home in Iraq.

One of my practices is reading and singing the sutra "Invoking Avalokiteshvara's Name" (music by Sister True Vow) to cultivate my capacity for deep listening and compassion. Avalokitesvara is the archetypal bodhisattva who embodies the great compassion of relieving suffering through deep listening and skillful action. I aspire to these qualities. I am reminded that the Chinese character for listening (聽) contains these elements: king of ears (耳王), ten eyes (十目), and one heart-mind (一心). In other words, in addition to listening with the best of our ears, we also use our eyes to observe with full attention, and we practice being present and receptive wholeheartedly.

Reflections on the Third Mindfulness Training and Contemplation: Liberating Boundless Love

Name: Melina Bondy/Chân Trăng Hải Ấn
Pronouns: they/them
Location: Tkaranto (Toronto, Canada)

When I was first introduced to the Five Mindfulness Trainings in 2003, I had no idea how deeply they would shape the course of my life. Among them, the Third Mindfulness

Training—centered on true love and sexual responsibility—both inspired and concerned me. Over the years, my relationship with this Training has shifted through different phases: as a new lay practitioner, as an experienced lay practitioner, as a monastic in the Plum Village tradition, and now again as a layperson. The Training's words have also changed. Looking back, I see how the practice has continually deepened and opened me in love, and by extension, evolved my practice.

My first reading of the Third Training left me inspired—except for one line. It spoke of sexual relations only within long-term commitments "made known to family and friends." I immediately thought: "They can't mean queer people." For many of us, visibility to family or society is unsafe or impossible. That phrase made me wonder whether the community was disconnected from queer realities—or even homophobic.

Yet I couldn't ignore the inspiration I felt from the rest of the Trainings. I went on a retreat with Thích Nhất Hạnh in 2005, where an LGBTQ group gave me the space to explore my inspiration and concerns with others who understood me. I initially resisted the Third Training, sensing that it carried the fragrance of religious persecution of gender and sexual minorities found elsewhere. But with the sangha eyes, I came to see its deeper spirit: cultivating true love, preventing harm, and engaging in radical honesty. As someone practicing polyamory, I realized that these values aligned with my commitment to transparency and genuine connection rather than socially prescribed norms. I realized that the Third Training could help me to love more deeply, and I decided to receive the full Five Mindfulness Trainings.

In the years that followed, I found new and creative ways to apply the Trainings in my life. At one point, I was in a committed relationship that aligned well with the external "form" of the Third Training. Yet when the call to monastic life arose, I was torn, even distressed. I loved my partner and knew I had to leave her in order to follow this calling, which seemed like the opposite of love.

During that painful transition, I turned to the Trainings nightly. They became my compass, not telling me exactly what to do but reminding me of my deepest aspiration: to act with honesty, reverence, and care for both myself and my partner. The Trainings showed me that staying in a relationship out of guilt or fear wasn't true love either. They helped me move through shame, and eventually, I was able to forgive myself and retain a friendship with my ex-partner. Life as a monastic brought me into a new relationship with the Third Training: celibacy. Initially, I feared how I would handle my sexual desires, which had often felt overwhelming in earlier years. But as a monastic, I was committed to working with, rather than acting from, sexual energy, and it evolved my practice again.

Rather than "letting go of attachment," which I realized still carried aversion, I learned to meet desire with mindfulness and kindness. Through body scans, inner child work, and compassion practices to give myself the attention I sought from others, I discovered that sexual energy also contained appreciation, beauty, and joy. What once felt like a force that controlled me became a source of freedom and even a doorway to greater, boundless love. I no longer feared my sexual energy—I was freed by it.

When I left monastic life for studies in somatic trauma therapy, I discovered yet another phase of practice with the Third Mindfulness Training. I recognized not only the need for mindfulness of the pull of sexual desire but also the deep mammalian need for safety, attention, and belonging known as the attachment system. I realized that while celibacy and monastic distance had been an excellent training ground, for me, in universal love, many of the triggers from familial and intimate relationships had not been touched in years. In returning to dating, I felt like an anxious teenager again. It was messy and confusing. My attachment system needed reawakening.

Just like the time when I took on celibacy in the monastery, dating in my late forties is again a time for creative practice. I found that, just as I learned to notice and befriend the hindrances (sensual desire, aversion, drowsiness, agitation, and doubt) in formal meditation, I could train myself to notice and befriend the evolutionary attachment patterns (secure, anxious, avoidant, and disorganized) as they showed up in my relationships. I could notice how these patterns related to the interpersonal and collective patterns of othering and belonging, as well as the possibility of true connection, belonging, and understanding.

Recently, this has been especially helpful as I've navigated a deep shock and heartbreak. When I notice that my anxious style takes over, I remind myself that I have secure patterns too. I remind myself that my lover's avoidance is a form of fearful self-protection, not just an attack on me. I prepare for our conversations with meditation on the Four

Brahmaviharas—friendliness, compassion, sympathetic joy, and equanimity—of true love. The insights of trauma theory and attachment science don't replace the Dharma but illuminate it, offering me tools to lessen aversion and deepen compassion as I try my best to remember my aspiration to love well, coupled or not.

Reflecting on this journey, I see that my practice with all the Trainings has changed over time, but the evolution has been most evident with the third one. While it may be challenging for some to talk about sexuality and desire, I am committed to doing so because honesty and integrity can free us. Monastic life trained me to love in the ultimate dimension of the Brahmaviharas, while lay life trains me to love in the historical dimension through ethics and wise action. My practice now is to weave these together—the impersonal cosmic love with the tender, imperfect, intimate love that makes us human.

Reflections on the Fourth Mindfulness Training and Contemplation: Reclaiming Deep Listening and Loving Speech

Name: Laura Alvarado/True Land of Reality
Pronouns: she/her
Location: Mexico City, Mexico

I was born and raised in Mexico City, and I am of Indigenous descent. My grandmother was born in Oaxaca and is of Mixtec descent, and my father was born in Mexico City and is of

P'urhépecha descent. My Indigenous culture and background were hidden and disavowed in my life because my parents were afraid I would be discriminated against.

I knew an important part of me was missing. I looked in the mirror and saw my beautiful features. I knew I was different, but I didn't understand how and couldn't recognize what was missing in my life. As it turns out, what was missing was my awareness and understanding of my Indigenous culture and roots. I have worked very hard to reclaim this important part of me and to acknowledge my roots, my culture, and my own sense of belonging.

I was honored to receive Lamp Transmission in Plum Village, France, in 2025. For me, as a Plum Village Dharma teacher, the Five Mindfulness Trainings and Contemplations are reminders to be fully aware of my suffering and the suffering of others, especially in my way of listening and speaking. The Trainings and Contemplations challenge me to go deeper in my understanding and to engage in loving speech and deep listening. I lost my Indigenous language because of how I was raised, and yet I speak Spanish, like nearly everyone in Mexico. But the question is: do we have understanding in how we communicate? Even though we all communicate in Spanish, we may at times take for granted that we fully understand each other. Practicing with the Trainings requires me to be careful and to ask questions that support understanding.

For me, Thầy's teaching on interbeing is powerful and is evident in my Indigenous culture. In Oaxacan culture, there is not a word for "I." Instead, "we" is the basic form of referring to individuals. This helps me understand that there is no happiness that is not related to another person, to "we." I am not complete without the other.

The essence of the Trainings and Contemplations is to be aware of my suffering and happiness and that of others. At times, I can inadvertently create suffering in my work as a psychologist advocating for children's rights. I catch myself making assumptions that others may or may not share. I am aware that my assumptions can be misguided, and this requires stopping and looking deeply.

The Trainings and Contemplations are not about perfection but are instead about being on a journey of understanding of this complex human experience. I don't relate to dos and don'ts, and the Trainings and Contemplations are not a set of strict rules. Instead, they guide me in what I do and say, pointing the way to live with peace, understanding, and compassion.

Reflections on the Fifth Mindfulness Training and Contemplation: Transforming Our Habits of Consumption

Name: Leslie Gordon/True Forest Sangha
Pronouns: he/him
Location: New York City

The Five Mindfulness Trainings, for me, are a living, breathing organism—a being with a life of its own. Conceived and given birth by the Buddha 2,600 years ago, this organism, like the sun, radiates warmth and life to all because of its universality and inclusiveness. It lives in reciprocity with the Four

Noble Truths, for together they offer a way to end suffering and attain liberation.

Like a hand whose fingers can each touch a note that together create an existential symphony, each Training resonates with and strengthens the others. Among these trainings, the Fifth Mindfulness Training on mindful consumption stands out as a beacon of awareness. It shines a spotlight on how our choices ripple through our minds, bodies, societies, and ecosystems.

The Fifth Training invites us to recognize the deep connection between well-being and the choices we make. Yet, in a culture steeped in instant gratification, conformity, and profit-driven values, mindfulness often becomes the exception rather than the norm. We are habituated to consume excessively—food, media, entertainment, even relationships—to cover our pain, loneliness, or fear. Instead of facing our suffering, we reach for distractions that numb rather than nourish.

I see this unmindful consumption reflected even in my grandchildren. They are often showered with too many toys, and before long, the novelty fades and the toys are discarded. Their focus shifts to screens, to iPads that command their attention so powerfully that simple human conversation becomes difficult. This, too, is the fruit of adult choices—a cycle of behavior that ripples through generations.

My Dharma name, True Forest Sangha, given to me by Thầy during my Order of Interbeing ordination at Magnolia Grove Monastery in 2011, speaks to the interbeing of all life. To live as True Forest Sangha is to understand that mindfulness is not an individual practice alone—it is an ecological, communal, and historical act. The Fifth Mindfulness Training calls us to act as custodians of this beautiful planet, to be mindful of the destruction of forests, the pollution of air and water, and the excesses of our consumer habits that feed climate change.

This awareness demands courage. It is not about proselytizing, but about educating ourselves, our families, and our communities on the rewards of consuming mindfully—food that nourishes, media that uplifts, and actions that heal.

When I reflect on the deeper roots of unmindful consumption, I return again and again to history—to colonialism. Our behaviors, as people of color, have been shaped by centuries of displacement and distortion. In precolonial times, our ancestors in Africa and the Caribbean lived in closer harmony with the earth. We ate natural foods, used herbs for healing, and respected the rhythms of life. Colonialism disrupted these ways, introducing exploitative systems that warped our sense of value and self-worth.

In Jamaica, where I grew up, I have witnessed how processed foods and sugar-heavy diets have replaced traditional, wholesome foods—leading to chronic illness, including diabetes, even among children. This is more than a dietary shift; it is a reflection of a deeper cultural displacement. Many people no longer cook at home. Instead, they spend their earnings on fast food—Kentucky Fried Chicken and Burger King—consuming convenience rather than care.

Even our sense of beauty and identity has been colonized. It saddens me to see brothers and sisters bleaching their skin, straightening their hair, and chasing standards of attractiveness rooted in Eurocentrism. Growing up, we learned Greek and Roman history but little of Africa's greatness. Egypt was rarely even described as part of Africa. Such erasures breed a quiet, corrosive self-hatred.

From colonial times to now, the message has been internalized: whiteness is superior; our natural selves are inferior. It is no wonder that even within our spiritual communities, traces of this conditioning persist. As Bob Marley sang, "Emancipate yourselves from mental slavery; none but ourselves can free our minds."

The Fifth Mindfulness Training gives us the tools to begin this emancipation. By bringing awareness to what we consume—not only food and drinks, but also ideas, histories, and self-images—we can begin to heal. When we see how colonialism has shaped our habits, our diets, our desires, and even our self-perception, we gain insight into why we consume to fill the void. With this understanding comes liberation: the possibility of choosing differently.

True mindfulness is revolutionary. It asks us to slow down in a world that profits from our distraction. It calls us to reclaim our ancestral wisdom, and to find healing not in what we buy or ingest, but in how we see and care for ourselves and one another.

We cannot change the past, but we can transform our relationship to it. Through the Fifth Mindfulness Training, we are invited to remember—to remember our connection to the earth, to our ancestors, and to the divine essence within. To consume mindfully is to live in reverence. It is to honor life itself.

Appendix

Dharma Resources

The Four Noble Truths

The Four Noble Truths and other key teachings of the Buddha are beautifully explored in depth by Thích Nhất Hạnh in his book *The Heart of the Buddha's Teaching.*

In the original translations of Buddhist teachings, the Four Noble Truths are referenced as the first teaching the Buddha gave after he realized enlightenment, or *nirvana*. This teaching is contextualized as setting the wheel of the Dharma in motion, ushering into that period a pathway to enlightenment realized by Shakyamuni Buddha.[24] We accept these truths as noble and virtuous because when realized, they lead to a noble or virtuous life, an awakened life of applied ethics, understanding, and love.

Each of these foundational truths carries with it a duty. The First Noble Truth, that suffering exists, is to be *investigated* and *understood or acknowledged*. In modern times, the Pali word (*dukkha*) and Sanskrit word (*duhkha*) are translated into English as suffering, unsatisfactoriness, or ill-being. All sentient beings are connected by the nature of a life span: once born, we will inevitably grow old, become sick, and pass away. Buddhist teachings encourage us to acknowledge the Five Remembrances: aging, illness, death, being separated from beings and things we care about, and creating our future life through our current intention and action. We can reflect on these Five Remembrances so as to minimize our suffering from them when they occur. We have great aversion to aging, illness, and death, which is our path by the nature of our being born. When we are unable to accept the inevitability of this mundane life course, living in ignorance, we suffer.

The Second Noble Truth tells us that there is a cause of suffering, or a path leading to suffering. The duty here is to *abandon* this cause or path, to abandon our ignorance. As noted about the practice of the Five Remembrances, if we abandon our fear or ignorance of aging, illness, and death, we will suffer less as they come to pass. Abandoning the cause of anything that brings us suffering begins to move us away from the effect.

As we abandon the cause or path of suffering, the Third Noble Truth—the cessation of suffering—is *realized* (the duty). Thích Nhất Hạnh referred to this cessation of suffering as a deep happiness or well-being (*sukha* in Pali and Sanskrit), the opposite of suffering or ill-being. Here we see the natural way the Four Noble Truths interact with each other in a cause and effect sequence. When we investigate and abandon the cause of ill-being, what is revealed is well-being; this means we find them both in each other when we look deeply.

The Fourth Noble Truth states that there is a path leading to the cessation of suffering, or to well-being, and the duty is to *develop* this path. While we abandon the causes of suffering (as suggested in the Second Noble Truth) to realize its cessation (as suggested in the Third Noble Truth), the Fourth Noble Truth provides a positive course to the cessation of suffering and to well-being. Returning to the Five Remembrances, this Fourth Noble Truth suggests we can develop a path that will help us stay in remembrance of the inevitability of aging, illness, and death. Therefore the Fourth Noble Truth points the way to developing a path to put an end to all our ill-being and to experience well-being and happiness. This path is referred to as the Noble Eightfold Path.

Buddhist teachings emphasize that these Four Noble Truths, when fully realized, can bring an end to all suffering.[25] They outline how we are to engage in the world in relation to phenomena to live a wholesome and ethical life and achieve happiness.[26]

The Noble Eightfold Path

The Noble Eightfold Path, which I also will refer to as the Path, is the way leading to well-being or happiness. According to the Fourth Noble Truth, we should develop the Path in order to reach the goal of well-being.[27] The eight elements, or factors, of the Path rely on each other and help one another to be fulfilled; they inter-are.

The first element of the Noble Eightfold Path is Right View. With Right View, we see the true nature of things. Right View allows us to go beyond dualistic perceptions of good and bad, right and wrong, same and different. We see that in the "good" thing, there is also something insufficient, something we might perceive as "bad," and vice versa: in the perceived "dirt," there exist seeds that will grow up and blossom into beautiful "flowers." This view allows us to see the interdependent nature of all phenomena. Right View brings this deep looking into each of the elements of the entire Noble Eightfold Path.

The next element is Right Intention, or Right Thinking. Right Thinking is a deeper thinking instructed by our Right View. It helps us see what is behind our habitual energies and determine how we will move forward to well-being. If our thoughts are judgmental or blaming, then our words and actions are likely to manifest judgment or blame. When we mindfully note what we are thinking, and assess whether we are bringing compassion and kindness into our thoughts, we can set our intention to change our way of thinking. This way of looking deeply helps us stay on the Path of happiness. When we notice our thinking is negative, we can keep looking to see why we have negative thoughts and elucidate the causes and conditions for them. We then resolve to transform the negative thoughts by understanding the causes.

The third element on the Path is Right Speech. With our view and resolve to act with compassion, we attempt to speak truthfully and kindly, using speech that brings benefit and nourishes our happiness as well as the happiness of others. We speak up when we see injustice, while assuring our speech is compassionate. Sometimes our speech might appear to be divisive in a space that does not have deep harmony. For example, imagine you are in a group of people where someone speaks negatively about another person who is from a different racial group than theirs, and no one says anything in response to the negative comment. You can find the right time to compassionately inquire into the reasons behind the person's unkind speech, without shame or blame. Their understanding may be lacking because of the conditions they grew up in, or perhaps they were forced to adapt this way of speaking. You can practice Right Speech to help them see the ignorance and harm in their thinking and words. You have the opportunity to minimize the violence from unmindful speech that brings harm to the person speaking and the people listening.

Because Right View allows us to see the nonseparation of all people, we can maintain an equanimous heart while helping others understand that although our mundane world is systematically structured to separate and discriminate by racial and ethnic identities, this is not Right View. When we practice using Right Speech in this way, helping others see the benefit of the Noble Eightfold Path, it leads to safety and happiness and brings great benefit to the world.

Right Action is the fourth element of the Noble Eightfold Path. Like Right Speech, Right Action is an attempt to act from a place of compassion. We are guided by our Right View and Right Thinking to assure that our actions are wholesome, and lead toward joy, and move us and those around us toward compassion. Some might ask if participating in a protest or rally against an authoritarian regime is Right Action. As practitioners on the Noble Eightfold Path, we have a responsibility to act with compassion and to reduce the likelihood of violence and war. When we stand up for peace and justice, we invite all into the net of nonseparation. Those engaging in war have a lot of ignorance that leads to their suffering and the suffering of others. They need other people's mindful speech and actions to help them wake up to their harmful actions. Our actions come from a place of understanding both the perpetrators of wars and those wanting to end wars. When we show up with compassion at such a rally, coming from a place of spaciousness and inclusivity, we are practicing Right Action—action that is advised by Right View and Right Thinking.

Right Livelihood, the fifth element on the Noble Eightfold Path, invites us to be mindful of the kind of work we do to support ourselves and our families. Does our work bring benefit? Finding work that helps us continue on our path of happiness is sometimes challenging. Because many of us live in countries that have racist, capitalist social and economic systems with militaristic values, sometimes we find ourselves in work that is harmful to ourselves and others. The result of such structures inevitably leads to social, wealth, housing, and health inequities. If we work for a factory that is manufacturing arms, and it's the only employment available, is this Right Livelihood? Thầy responded to similar questions by suggesting that if we bring our Right Mindfulness into these spaces, we may be one of the few people bringing some benefit. If we work for institutions of higher learning where there is tremendous income disparity, is this Right Livelihood? We can consider engaging in actions that help minimize the disparity. Right Action invites us to address how we can move toward more adequate work compensation for all, through a redistribution of pay and benefits. Right View must guide us in discerning our Right Action.

Along with Right View, the sixth element of Right Effort is the guardian of our thinking, speech, and action. Also known as Right Diligence, Right Effort helps us to be aware of what we are about to think, say, and do. We assess whether our thoughts, speech, and actions are wholesome or unwholesome, and we make every effort to prevent and remove the unwholesome while maintaining and increasing the wholesome. We become aware of what is hindering our wholesome behaviors and what is nourishing them. The five hindrances of Buddhism are sensual desire, aversion, sloth and torpor (dullness and drowsiness), restlessness and worry, and delusion/ignorance. With mindfulness, Right Diligence guards our mind so that when any of these hindrances arise, we are ready to prevent or remove and replace them. We can practice with antidotes to the hindrances. For example, if we have severe pain in one part of our body and are caught in despair and fear that it will not change, we can remember that all phenomena are impermanent, so the pain will change. We also can remind ourselves that other parts of our body are not in pain. If we tend toward having an angry or irritated personality, we can notice this habit energy, and with Right Effort, develop practices that bring forth loving kindness. We slowly gain understanding as we notice how others treat us when we are more kind and compassionate. If we notice that we have lots of doubt about our spiritual practice, we can make an effort to practice regularly to discern through our own experience if the practice brings us happiness.

The seventh element on the Path is Right Mindfulness. All of the elements rely on each other, and Right Mindfulness keeps us aware of each of them. For example, mindfulness helps us notice which hindrances are present so we can practice diligently, which thoughts nourish happiness, and which thoughts deplete us and nourish our hindrances. Right

Mindfulness keeps us in awareness of our speech and actions. We cannot choose if we are not mindful that there is a choice to be made. By practicing to be mindful of our body and our breath, we begin to notice the connection between our thinking and its effects on our body. We learn how to breathe slowly to bring calm to our body.

Mindfulness of our feelings and sensations helps us notice what is pleasant, unpleasant, or neutral when our senses make contact with an object. Our mindfulness helps us to notice our tendency to move away from things we perceive as unpleasant and move toward or desire things we perceive to be pleasant. Mindfulness of our perceptions and mental formations helps us to note how our mind proliferates stories after we make contact with an object of the senses. For example, our ears hear a birdsong and we think of a pleasant situation in the past when we heard a similar birdsong. Mindfulness of our consciousness helps us to have bare awareness of the object of our senses before mental proliferation occurs. In this way, we become aware of how we attach narratives to the objects of our mind.

This bare awareness of Right Mindfulness leads to Right Concentration, the eighth element of the Path. Right Concentration quiets the proliferation of the mind, bringing a one-pointed focus to the object. This focus allows us to see clearly what is there in front of us, without stories from the past or projections into the future. The heightened focus allows a clear seeing, a clarity that is simple and direct. The debris or stories surrounding the object go out of focus, and our mind brings the object into greater focus, holding bare awareness of it. The stillness of the mind, concentrated through Right Mindfulness, allows a clear comprehension. This clear seeing leads to insight, or wisdom, about the object of concentration.

Through these eight elements, which support and at times lead to each other, a path to insight is developed. In this way, the Fourth Noble Truth, the path leading to happiness and well-being, is achieved through the practice of the Noble Eightfold Path.

The Four Establishments of Mindfulness

The teachings contained in The Discourse on the Establishment of Mindfulness (the Sattipatthana Sutra) are fundamental to the practice of Buddhist meditation. The sutra has been studied, practiced, and handed down with care from generation to generation since the time of the Buddha, for 2,500 years. They address mindfulness of the body, mindfulness of the feelings, mindfulness of the mind, and mindfulness of the objects of the mind. In his book *Transformation and Healing*,[28] Thích Nhất Hạnh presents his translation of the Discourse on the Establishment of Mindfulness along with his commentary and twenty-three exercises and contemplations to aid in the practice of mindfulness in daily life. You may also find the translation on the Plum Village website.[29]

The Six Paramitas

The word *paramita* translates to "perfection," in the sense of "wholeness" or "completeness," in Buddhism, referring to a noble quality cultivated and embodied by a bodhisattva. We can meditate on these qualities and practice to embody them in our lives. The Five Mindfulness Trainings, the second paramita, offer a foundation for the quality of *sila,* and they are interwoven with all of the perfections:

Giving (dana)
Mindfulness trainings (sila)
Inclusiveness (ksanti)
Diligence (virya)
Meditation (dhyana)
Insight (prajna)

The first paramita, the first door of action, is *dana,* giving and generosity. The second door of action is *sila,* the precepts, the mindfulness trainings, and guidelines for ethical behavior. The third door is *ksanti,* all-embracing inclusiveness. The fourth door of action is *virya,* diligence, energy, effort, and steadfastness in the practice. The fifth is *dhyana,* meditation, the practice of stopping and calming and looking deeply. The sixth is *prajna,* wisdom and understanding.

Thích Nhất Hạnh says:

> The Sanskrit term "paramita" is usually translated in English as "perfection," but in Chinese Buddhist literature it is always rendered in a character that translates literally as "crossing to the other shore." The six paramitas are very concrete means for us to cross over the sea of suffering to the shore of freedom from craving, anger, envy, despair, and delusion. Through cultivating and perfecting these six ways of being, we can reach the other shore very quickly—it may take only a few seconds

for us to cross over the river of suffering and arrive on the shore of well-being. We may have thought that it would take many years of practice in order to get free of the afflictions but if we know how to cultivate and manifest these six qualities, we can cross over right here and now.

All of the great bodhisattvas manifest the qualities of the six paramitas in various ways, and each of these six doors of action exists in interdependence with the others. In any one of these six qualities, you can see the other five. This is the approach that we should always take when we study and practice Buddhism, because the very foundation of Buddhist wisdom is interbeing—the one contains the all.

It is very important that we understand the nature of interbeing of the six paramitas. By practicing shila [sila], the mindfulness trainings, you are also practicing giving. When you know how to live mindfully, you are offering something very meaningful to the world. The practice of inclusiveness is also a practice of giving. When you fully accept people, embrace them, and take care of them, it is a great gift. Through the practice of embracing and caring for others you help bring about more peace and stability in your family and community. The practices of diligence and meditation also bring a lot of joy, stability, transformation, and healing not only to yourself but also to those around you.

And the practice of prajña offers the kind of understanding and wisdom that can help all of us cross over the river of suffering to the shore of liberation. The six paramitas are an essential practice of the bodhisattva path. In order to manifest ourselves in the dimension of action and serve most effectively as the arms and hands of the Buddhas and bodhisattvas in the world, we practice to cultivate and perfect these six qualities within ourselves. The moment we see the presence of all the paramitas in each paramita, we will begin to fully realize and truly live the practice.[30]

The Five Spiritual Powers

Valerie:

In 2003, I received the Fourteen Mindfulness Trainings from Thích Nhất Hạnh, who gave me the Dharma name True Power of the Sangha. I was one of a group of about fifteen people who received the Trainings at Stonehill College in Easton, Massachusetts. As Thầy read my Dharma name, there was an audible gasp in the audience. After the ceremony, Sister Chân Đức (True Virtue) approached me to remind me that the word *power* in the Plum Village tradition doesn't have the conventional meaning of power. I was puzzled.

In 2018, when I received Lamp Transmission in Plum Village, France, my Dharma name was changed to True Sangha Power. The change seemed minor, but it had a significant impact. For me, it was about redefining what power meant in my life.

Before this, I thought of power as individually centered. I believed power was my own personal achievement, my ambition, being "in charge," creating a vision of a future outcome and then developing my own latent abilities and driving toward a successful outcome. As a lawyer and lobbyist, I was driven by this quest for conventional power.

Most of my life, long before I started practicing mindfulness meditation, people have called me "strong and powerful."

I was curious about this and began to look deeper into my own identity. I recalled a story my mother had told me about how I received my name. When my mother was giving birth to me, she asked the woman in the hospital bed next to her what name she was giving to her daughter, and the woman said, "Valerie." My mother said she liked that name and hence, I got my name. After many years of people saying they thought I was so strong and so powerful, which was hard for me to see and understand, I decided to look up the definition of my name. I came to understand that my name means "strong," "healthy," or "brave," and is derived from the Latin word *valere* (to be strong). Suddenly, things made sense. I realized that the individual power that others naturally saw in me, which I had unconsciously cultivated through my legal career, was a certain kind of power that was gifted to me at birth, and that on my spiritual path, I was being called into a different kind of power. I began to understand that much of my life had been spent craving and pursuing power—as in status, money, ambition, recognition—and the pursuit left me drained, soulless, and lonely. For years, I held a nagging feeling that no matter what I achieved, nothing would be enough. I harbored a constant, low-grade sense of hypervigilance, pushing myself to do more and to be better. I realized my definition of power didn't include spaciousness to be happy, to be free from anxiety and a competitive drive.

Thầy's teachings on the Five Spiritual Powers have truly helped me to live into a different understanding of power that has affected my livelihood, my relationships with myself and others, and my role as a Dharma teacher. Thầy distinguishes between true power and cravings, and I see now that I was caught in cravings, not practicing true spiritual power. In the Plum Village tradition, power is a spiritual path that has five elements: faith, diligence, mindfulness, concentration, and insight. I will briefly describe each.

The Power of Faith

In *The Art of Power,* Thích Nhất Hạnh describes faith as a path that leads to liberation.[31] It is a sense of internal confidence and trust in our capacity to transform and heal. This type of faith is powerful, and it is the fruit of practice. With the wisdom of interbeing, we understand that the energies of understanding and compassion are inherent in each person, and this supports the energy of confidence.

The Power of Diligence

Thầy describes diligence as the power to remember and re-engage your best self, your *bodhicitta* vows, for your own and societal well-being and transformation. There are four elements of diligence. The first is to practice "selective watering," meaning to expose yourself to wholesome and positive elements as much as possible. Given the troubling times we are in, this may be hard to do. However, we can be mindful of what and how much we are consuming from social media, difficult conversations, and our environment, and as much as possible, allow for the positive in our lives.

The second aspect of diligence is calming and replacing afflictive emotions with positive emotions. Thầy says the longer afflictive emotions remain in our consciousness, the stronger they become, but we can replace them with something positive, like listening to beautiful music that generates feelings of calm or going for a walk to help us feel a quality of balance and wellness.[32]

The third aspect of diligence is to learn ways to proactively engage what is nourishing and healing, such as walking in a beautiful place or speaking with a friend. These actions can help manifest the positive.[33]

The fourth and final aspect of diligence is to retain positive mind states for as long as possible by continually cultivating these states of mind throughout the day.[34]

The Power of Mindfulness

Mindfulness is the third spiritual power. Life can only be lived in the present; the past is gone, and the future is not yet here. In the rush and tumble of daily life, we can forget this basic reality. With the power of awareness in the present moment, we can generate within ourselves the capacity to encounter things as they are. We can recognize, embrace, and take care of our suffering. We can cultivate freedom from anxiety and worry over projects and work. And we can enjoy our life.

The Power of Concentration

With mindfulness, concentration is present, and this is the fourth element of spiritual power. This power allows us to look deeply and develop a mindset of curiosity, inquiry, and radical lifelong learning. With this power, we become aware of the impermanence of life, and with this awareness, we can begin to understand what is most important and meaningful.[35]

The Power of Insight

The fifth spiritual power is insight, which is a kind of understanding. With the power of concentration and looking deeply, we grow understanding. Insight arises from an environment of mindfulness and concentration. Thầy has called insight a superpower. As we touch insight, we touch the liberating power of impermanence and interbeing.[36]

I continue to live into Thầy's teachings on spiritual power with compassion and understanding.

The Four Immeasurables

The Four Immeasurables are also called the Four Immeasurable Minds of Love—and the Four Divine Abodes—because if you practice them, your mind of love will grow in you every day until it embraces the whole world. In his book about the Four Immeasurables, *Teachings on Love*, Thích Nhất Hạnh says, "You will become happier, and everyone around you will become happier . . . . When you love because living beings need your love, not because someone belongs to your family, your nation, or your religion, then you are loving without discrimination and practicing true love."[37]

The Four Immeasurable Minds are the four elements of true love:

1. Loving kindness, *maitri* (the desire to offer happiness)
2. Compassion, *karuna* (the desire to remove suffering from others)

3. Sympathetic joy, *mudita* (the desire to bring joy to people around you, and allowing their happiness to bring you joy)
4. Equanimity, *upeksha* (the desire to accept everything and not to discriminate)

When true love is present, it preserves your freedom and the freedom of your beloved. The fourth Immeasurable, equanimity, is key in not making a prison of our love for ourselves and others. Thích Nhất Hạnh says, "The fourth element of true love is *upeksha,* which means equanimity, nonattachment, nondiscrimination, even-mindedness, or letting go."

> Upeksha has the mark called *samatajnana,* "the wisdom of equality," the ability to see everyone as equal, not discriminating between ourselves and others. In a conflict, even though we are deeply concerned, we remain impartial, able to love and to understand both sides. We shed all discrimination and prejudice, and remove all boundaries between ourselves and others. As long as we see ourselves as the one who loves and the other as the one who is loved, as long as we value ourselves more than others or see others as different from us, we do not have true equanimity. We have to put ourselves "into the other person's skin" and become one with him if we want to understand and truly love him. When that happens, there is no "self' and no "other."[38]

Notes

1 Seth G. Jones and Riley McCabe, "Russia's Battlefield Woes in Ukraine," Center for Strategic and International Studies, June 3, 2025. https://www.csis.org/analysis/russias-battlefield-woes-ukraine.

2 "Number of Palestinian and Israeli Casualties Caused by the Israel-Hamas War 2023–2026," Statista, February 2, 2026, https://www.statista.com/statistics/1422308/palestinian-territories-israel-number-fatalities-and-injuries-caused-by-the-israel-and-hamas-war/.

3 Andrea Hsu, "Officially, 59,000 federal jobs are gone under Trump. There's more to the picture," NPR, *All Things Considered,* June 6, 2025, https://www.npr.org/2025/06/04/nx-s1-5421277/trump-federal-workers-layoffs-doge.

4 Michael Barbaro, host, *The Daily*, podcast, "How Trump Upended 60 Years of Civil Rights," New York Times Podcasts, October 21, 2025, https://www.youtube.com/watch?v=epVxOkN14Wg. See also New York City Bar Association, "Statement on the Trump Administration's Attack on Civil Rights, June 2, 2025, https://www.nycbar.org/reports/statement-on-the-trump-administrations-attacks-on-civil-rights.

5 The Arthapada Sutra, chapter 16, equivalent to Sutta Nipata 935–954. *Sutras* are transcribed texts or scriptures of the oral teachings of the Buddha.

6 Valerie Brown and Marisela B. Gomez, MD, "The Path of Racial and Social Equity: An Open Heart Is Called for Now" in *The Mindfulness Bell,* no. 70 (October 2015); https://www.parallax.org/mindfulnessbell/article/the-path-of-racial-and-social-equity/.

7 Thích Nhất Hạnh, *For a Future to Be Possible: Buddhist Ethics for Everyday Life* (Parallax Press, 2007), 64–65.

8 Nhất Hạnh, *For a Future to Be Possible,* 76–77.

9 Nhất Hạnh, *For a Future to Be Possible,* 74.

10 Thích Nhất Hạnh, "The Deeper Meaning Behind Monastic Rules," Plum Village website, January 13, 2022, https://plumvillage.org/articles/the-deeper-meaning-behind-monastic-rules.

11 Thích Nhất Hạnh, *Cracking the Walnut: Understanding the Dialectics of Nagarjuna* (Palm Leaves Press, 2023), 224.

12 Nhất Hạnh, *Cracking the Walnut,* 203.

13 Thích Nhất Hạnh, *The Other Shore: A New Translation of the Heart Sutra with Commentaries* (Palm Leaves Press, 2017), 27.

14 "The Five Mindfulness Trainings," Plum Village website, https://plumvillage.org/mindfulness/the-5-mindfulness-trainings. Revised June 15, 2022.

15 National Employment Law Project, "New Report Finds Amazon Warehouse Wages Fall Far Short, Fail to Provide Workers Middle-Income Earnings." September 26, 2023. https://www.nelp.org/new-report-finds-amazon-warehouse-wages-fall-far-short-fail-to-provide-workers-middle-income-earnings.

16 Robin Wall Kimmerer, *Braiding Sweetgrass: Indigenous Wisdom, Scientific Knowledge and the Teachings of Plants* (Milkweed Editions, 2013), 175–201.

17 Thích Nhất Hạnh, *Transformation and Healing: Sutra on the Four Establishments of Mindfulness* Second Edition (Parallax Press, 2002). The teachings contained in The Discourse on the Establishment of Mindfulness (the Sattipatthana Sutra) are fundamental to the practice of Buddhist meditation. The sutra has been studied, practiced, and handed down with care from generation to generation since the time of the Buddha, for 2,500 years. They address mindfulness of the body, mindfulness of the feelings, mindfulness of the mind, and mindfulness of the objects of the mind. In his book *Transformation and Healing,* Thích Nhất Hạnh presents his translation of the Discourse on the Establishment of Mindfulness along with his commentary and twenty-three exercises and contemplations to aid in the practice of mindfulness in daily life. You may also find the translation on the Plum Village website. "Discourse on the Four Establishments of Mindfulness," Plum Village website, translated by Thích Nhất Hạnh from the Satipaṭṭhāna Sutta, Majjhima Nikāya 10, https://plumvillage.org/library/sutras/discourse-on-the-four-establishments-of-mindfulness.

18 Thích Nhất Hạnh, *The Admonitions and Encouraging Words of Master Guishan* (Palm Leaves Press, 2022), 50–53.

19 Viktor Frankl, "Free to Be Human," Viktor Frankl Institute of Logotherapy in Israel, https://themeaningseeker.org/free-to-be-human. Accessed April 28, 2026.

20 Dr. Howard Thurman, "Baccalaureate Address at Spelman College," May 4, 1980. Edited by Jo Moore Stewart. *The Spelman Messenger* 96, no. 4 (Summer 1980), 14–15.

21 Wendy Johnson, *Gardening at the Dragon's Gate: At Work in the Wild and Cultivated World* (Bantam Dell, 2008).

22 Nhất Hạnh, *For a Future to Be Possible,* 8.

23 Upadatta Sutta, SN 45.2. Also see David Viafora, "Spiritual Friendship Is the Path," in *Buddhadharma* magazine, Fall 2021, available on the *Lion's Roar* website, https://www.lionsroar.com/spiritual-friendship-is-the-path/.

24 Thích Nhất Hạnh, *The Heart of the Buddha's Teachings: Transforming Suffering into Peace, Joy, and Liberation* (Harmony Books, 1999).

25 Bhikkhu Bodhi, *Noble Truths, Noble Path: The Heart Essence of the Buddha's Original Teachings* (Wisdom Publications, 2023).

26 Marisela B. Gomez, Antoinette González, Kim Fleisher, Lori A. Perine, Victoria Mausisa, and Y. L. Renita Wong, "Practicing with The Four Noble Truths in the World," *The Mindfulness Bell,* February 5, 2024, https://www.parallax.org/mindfulnessbell/article/practicing-with-the-four-noble-truths-in-the-world.

27 Nhất Hạnh, *The Heart of the Buddha's Teachings*; Bhikkhu Bodhi, *The Noble Eightfold Path: Way to the End of Suffering* (Pariyatti Press, 2006).

28 Thích Nhất Hạnh, *Transformation and Healing: Sutra on the Four Establishments of Mindfulness* Second Edition (Parallax Press, 2002).

29 "Discourse on the Four Establishments of Mindfulness," Plum Village website, translated by Thích Nhất Hạnh from the Satipaṭṭhāna Sutta, Majjhima Nikāya 10, https://plumvillage.org/library/sutras/discourse-on-the-four-establishments-of-mindfulness.

30 Thích Nhất Hạnh, *Opening the Heart of the Cosmos: Insights on the Lotus Sutra* (Parallax Press, 2003), 176.

31 Thích Nhất Hạnh, *The Art of Power* (HarperOne, 2008), 15–16.
32 Nhất Hạnh, *The Art of Power*, 19–20.
33 Nhất Hạnh, *The Art of Power*, 20–21.
34 Nhất Hạnh, *The Art of Power*, 21–22.
35 Nhất Hạnh, *The Art of Power*, 23–24.
36 Nhất Hạnh, *The Art of Power*, 24–29.
37 Thích Nhất Hạnh, *Teachings on Love* (Parallax Press, 1997), 2.
38 Nhất Hạnh, *Teachings on Love* (Parallax Press, 1997), 8–9.

Acknowledgments

We would like to acknowledge and offer heartfelt gratitude and respect to our dear teacher Zen Master Thầy Thích Nhất Hạnh (*Thầy* in Vietnamese means "teacher"), the legendary monk, author, and peace activist. Thầy cofounded the Plum Village Community of Engaged Buddhism and shared an accessible, practical Dharma with the world through his many teachings, practices, and writing. Although Thầy passed in 2022, he continues to be present in all his disciples, both monastic and lay practitioners. It is through the continued practice and sharing of the teachings that his students can assure Thầy will continue to live beautifully into the future. We acknowledge dear Sister Chan Khong, cofounder of the Plum Village Community of Engaged Buddhism. Sister Chan Khong is a continuation of Thầy and the gentle, grounded, and powerful practices of our tradition. Her demeanor reminds us that peacemaking in the world begins with peacemaking inside ourselves. We acknowledge too the worldwide community of monastic and lay practitioners who support these teachings and legacy.

Valerie Brown:

Writing is a birthing process, and it takes place in relationship. This book could not have been written without the care, love, and support of many people. I want to thank Dr. Marisela B. Gomez for her spiritual friendship, support, love, care, and understanding over many years. In writing this book, we traveled many paths together, and I am incredibly grateful for each and every step. I want to thank my spiritual friends Kaira Jewel Lingo; Drs. Larry Ward and Peggy Rowe-Ward; Roshi Joan Halifax, Kodo Noah Roen, and Dr. Wendy Lau of Upaya Zen Center; the Hemera Foundation; Viviane Ephraimson-Abt and her partner, Paul; and the entire Colorado Plum Village sanghas for their support during the Crestone, Colorado, retreat. I am grateful to Frances and George Rhoads, who offered their beautiful lake cabin that allowed me the time and space to complete this book. I wish to acknowledge the Quaker community and especially Pendle Hill Retreat and Study Center in Wallingford, Pennsylvania, and Francisco Burgos and Frances Kreimer for their support and commitment to social justice and radical hospitality. Thank you especially to my family: Katie Brown; her partner, Jose; their children Evelyn, Sophia, and Machi; my brother Lloyd; and my friends Karen Erlichman, Marcia Lee, Sharon Victor, Abraham Liebson, and Elli Weisbaum for their consistent presence and support. Finally, thank you to the monastics of the worldwide Plum Village sanghas, especially those residing at Plum Village in France and at Blue Cliff Monastery and Deer Park Monastery and Magnolia Grove Monastery in the United States. Thank you too to all those who read early drafts of the book and offered endorsements. Gratitude to Sister Chân Đức, Ruth King, Tara Brach, Rhonda V. Magee, Sister Peace, Kazu Haga, Zenju Earthlyn Manuel, Larry Yang, Kaira Jewel Lingo, Larry

Ward and Peggy Rowe-Ward, Wendy Dainin Lau, Pamela Ayo Yetunde, Chan Teacher Guogu, Chris Mohr, Heather Lyn Mann, Valerie Mason-John, Dzung X. Vo, Jack Lawlor, Dori Middleman, Yuk-Lin Renita Wong, Lyn Fine, Mark A. Putnam, eli tizcareño ortiz, Brother Pháp Lưu, Sister Bội Nghiêm, and many others for their loving support of this book. This book would not be possible without the deep commitment and tireless support of Parallax Press. We deeply appreciate the work of editors Natascha Bruckner and Hisae Matsuda and all the staff at Parallax Press: Katie Eberle, Erin Wiegand, Maureen Forys, Katie Sheehan, Liz McKellar, Jess Brown, Jacopo Miceli, Tony Lulek, John Matsuoka, Leslie Schneider, and publisher Matt Friberg.

Marisela B. Gomez:

My aspiration for a path of liberation began with my grandmother, aunt, and mother. These were the women I saw choosing to live a life beyond the one society prescribed to them. They remain my teachers forever; I love them. I offer a heartfelt and deep bow of love and gratitude to my coauthor, spiritual friend, mentor, and fellow outdoor enthusiast Valerie Brown. Practicing on this path of freedom requires many types of spiritual friendship. We need someone to be our bell of mindfulness when we forget to practice, and for me, this person is Valerie. She has her eyes set for the long road that will lead to liberation while she constantly looks deeply at the daily path that gets her there. The support from Parallax Press has been unending: Hisae Matsuda remains open and ready to assure that our community of practice includes everyone who suffers—and that is all of us. Deep gratitude to our Plum Village Community of Engaged Buddhism and the centers across the world that continue our lineage, showing the way to our liberation. I acknowledge and offer a deep bow to the community of monastic and lay practitioners at Blue Cliff Monastery in Pine Bush, New York, US. Deep gratitude to the sanghas I engage with regularly, spiritual friends on this path of individual and collective liberation: Baltimore and Beyond Mindfulness Community, the ARISE (Awakening through Race, Intersectionality, and Social Equity) Sangha, and Kaira Jewel Lingo and the Garrison Institute BIPOC (Black, Indigenous, and other People of Color) Sangha. This path continues to blossom spiritual friends, each teaching me about love and liberation. Their heartfelt and steady spiritual practice and commitment keeps me on this path. To Baltimore folk, my newly and long term beloveds, who keep me on the path of justice and liberation, reminding me that all our suffering demands transformation, I bow deeply in gratitude. I acknowledge the Village of Love and Resistance (VOLAR), whose deep work of manifesting liberation through justice and joy schools me in staying grounded in practice as we collectively transform our suffering; we are rebuilding with love. Each person in my life teaches me about kindness and this nourishes my *bodhicitta*—my source of love—endlessly. I bow in deep gratitude.

About the Authors

Valerie Brown, JD, transformed her twenty-year, high-pressure career as a lawyer-lobbyist into human-scale, social equity-centered work, guiding leaders and organizations to foster greater understanding, authenticity, compassion, and trust. She was ordained as a Dharma teacher in Thích Nhất Hạnh's Plum Village tradition of Engaged Buddhism and is a member of the Religious Society of Friends (Quakers). Visit valerie-brown.us to discover more about her books and teaching.

Marisela B. Gomez, MD, is a cofounder of the cooperative community Village of Love and Resistance in Baltimore, Maryland, US, organizing for power, healing, and the reclamation of land. She is a meditation teacher, physician-scientist, and holistic health practitioner. She is the author of *Race, Class, Power, and Organizing in East Baltimore* and coauthor of *Healing Our Way Home*, along with other scholarly, political, and spiritual writings. https://www.mariselabgomez.com/

Monastics and visitors practice the art of mindful living in the tradition of Thich Nhat Hanh at our mindfulness practice centers around the world. To reach any of these communities, or for information about how individuals, couples, and families can join in a retreat, please contact:

PLUM VILLAGE
24240 Thénac, France
plumvillage.org

LA MAISON DE L'INSPIR
77510 Villeneuve-sur-Bellot, France
maisondelinspir.org

HEALING SPRING MONASTERY
77510 Verdelot, France
healingspringmonastery.org

MAGNOLIA GROVE MONASTERY
Batesville, MS 38606, USA
magnoliagrovemonastery.org

BLUE CLIFF MONASTERY
Pine Bush, NY 12566, USA
bluecliffmonastery.org

DEER PARK MONASTERY
Escondido, CA 92026, USA
deerparkmonastery.org

EUROPEAN INSTITUTE OF APPLIED BUDDHISM
D-51545 Waldbröl, Germany
eiab.eu

THAILAND PLUM VILLAGE
Nakhon Ratchasima
30130 Thailand
thaiplumvillage.org

ASIAN INSTITUTE OF APPLIED BUDDHISM
Lantau Island, Hong Kong
pvfhk.org

STREAM ENTERING MONASTERY
Porcupine Ridge, Victoria 3461
Australia
nhapluu.org

MOUNTAIN SPRING MONASTERY
Bilpin, NSW 2758, Australia
mountainspringmonastery.org

For more information visit: *plumvillage.org*
To find an online sangha visit: *plumline.org*
For more resources, try the Plum Village app: *plumvillage.app*
Social media: *@thichnhathanh @plumvillagefrance*

THICH NHAT HANH FOUNDATION

planting seeds of Compassion

THE THICH NHAT HANH FOUNDATION works to continue the mindful teachings and practices of Zen Master Thich Nhat Hanh in order to foster peace and transform suffering in all people, animals, plants, and our planet. Through donations to the Foundation, thousands of generous supporters ensure the continuation of Thich Nhat Hanh's vision and help care for practice centers and monastics around the world. Your gifts help bring transformative practices to people who otherwise could not access them and support local mindfulness initiatives that ease suffering and cultivate joy.

By becoming a supporter, you join thousands of others committed to learning about, embodying, and sharing the life-changing practices of mindfulness, loving speech, deep listening, and compassion for oneself, each other, and the world.

For more information on how you can help spread Thich Nhat Hanh's teachings and practices globally, and to subscribe to our newsletters offering teachings, news, and information about retreats, please visit tnhf.org.

PARALLAX PRESS, a nonprofit publisher founded by Zen Master Thich Nhat Hanh, publishes books and media on the art of mindful living and Engaged Buddhism. We are committed to offering teachings that help transform suffering and injustice. Our aspiration is to contribute to collective insight and awakening, bringing about a more joyful, healthy, and compassionate society.

View our entire library at parallax.org.

THE MINDFULNESS BELL is a journal of the art of mindful living in the Plum Village tradition of Thich Nhat Hanh. To subscribe or to see the worldwide directory of Sanghas (local mindfulness groups), visit mindfulnessbell.org.